Maria Lancaster's book, *Souls on Ice*, digs deep into the freezer where life is waiting and shares heartwarming stories of real families and the awe-inspiring second chance every adoption allows for the frozen embryo population. You will come away knowing the precious *souls on ice* deserve and urgently need a rescue and how life transforming that rescue can be. Who better to lead us into the revolutionizing truth of the incredible experience of adopting a frozen embryo than my friend Maria! Meeting Maria and Elisha at a mutual speaking event in Colorado Springs with Dr. James Dobson is one of the highlights of my life. We snuck away for a personal visit and some fun playtime for Elisha and Gracie. During our recent radio interview, Maria's sentences danced with uplifting and empowering stories. Now those stories and more are in this book. Grab a hanky because these compelling stories testify to the miracles God can perform through willing hearts. The Bible teaches us to take care of the orphans. This book will show you an extraordinary way of doing just that. It is a little taste of heaven and the results of the amazing work God has accomplished through Maria! The world is a better place because of the awareness Maria has brought to the dear and many *souls on ice*. This book will warm up the world to adopting frozen embryos, and that is a win/win for everyone!

Diane Dike, Ph.D.
Foster/adoptive mom, author, speaker, singer
President/founder of Second Chance with Saving Grace
Host of the Dr. Diane Dike Radio Show
www.DianeDike.org

What should be done with the remaining embryos from IVF? Who do they belong to? Is it better to leave them frozen as *souls on ice* or to thaw them and let them die a natural death or to donate them to be destroyed to generate embryonic stem cells for research? Maria Lancaster's dream of a true "adoption" program for those frozen embryos provides food for thought and poignant answers to these questions that have been fiercely debated. *Souls on Ice* shows us that they belong to their parents, not to scientists; that they are children waiting for a home, not property to be screened and selected, sold or donated for destruction; and that God alone can turn bad into good by using these frozen babies to answer a couple's deepest desire to have a child. Participating in the real-life story of one of the couples in this book turned my scientifically based opposition to embryo-destroying research into a deeper spiritual opposition to the trafficking and destruction of another human being for biomedical research and changed my life forever.

Theresa A. Deisher, Ph.D.
President & CEO, AVM Biotechnology
Seattle, Washington
www.avmbiotech.com

Who can resist a real-life story with a happy ending? This collection of true lives, through the battle of infertility to the manifest HOPE embryo adoption offers, is evidence of our gracious God's creative work. He is always for life, and the proof is in these pages. You will experience a great anticipation as you read the journeys of these families. Then profound joy and wonder come into their stories, best found in a newborn's arrival to an eager mom and dad. Maria Lancaster works faithfully, as well as prayerfully, in this life-giving assignment from God to foster life through embryo adoption. Couldn't we all use a lot more hope, joy and wonder? *Souls on Ice* will inform and inspire!

Lisa Crump
Senior director, National Day of Prayer Task Force
www.nationaldayofprayer.org

I knew Maria before she married Jeff Lancaster, though the paths of our lives took different roads. After the passing of my husband, Reverend Dennis Bennett, in 1991, I gratefully discovered that Maria, a former parishioner, was taking flowers to his grave! Now, after birthing her own miracle baby, Elisha, and co-founding Embryo Adoption Services of Cedar Park in 2008, Maria is helping to bring life to near-death frozen embryos. I recommend you read this amazing, heartwarming, hope-building book of new miracles that could only happen in this 21st century.

Dr. Rita Bennett, M.A., Litt.D.
www.emotionallyfree.org

My husband, Dr. Greg Romine, and I have devoted our lives to rescuing innocent children from the terrible plight of human sex trafficking. Likewise, our good friends Jeff and Maria Lancaster have devoted their lives to the plight of the "abandoned" human frozen embryo. The little unseen lives waiting for a family number in the hundreds of thousands. While it is impossible to rescue them all, we must do all we can to inform and educate society that a frozen embryo is human life, deserving of rescue. *Souls on Ice* will touch you, move you, change you and challenge you to reconsider your views of the value of an "unseen" life. Their daughter's life changed our lives. I hope Elisha's story and those of other families in this "first-of-its-kind" collection of miracles will give you hope and faith that there is a God who cares about the smallest details of our lives.

Dr. Cyndi Romine
Director and CEO, Called To Rescue
Vancouver, Washington
www.calledtorescue.org

There was *Schindler's List*, and now there is "Maria Lancaster's List." The world dean of geneticists, the late Dr. Jerome Lejeune of Paris, France, testifying in the Tennessee frozen human embryo case in 1989, spoke of very tiny human beings as human embryos compacted by the hundreds in a "concentration can" of liquid nitrogen. The French press mistook it and printed it as "concentration camp." Dr. Lejeune commented that it was a curious mistake because a concentration can is something that was invented to terribly slow down life, whereas a concentration camp is something that was invented to terribly speed up death. He added: "In either case, the wall imprisons innocents."

Martin Palmer
Pro-life attorney and advocate for the equal humanity
and personhood of preborn children
Founder of the National Association for the
Advancement of Preborn Children

Souls on Ice is history literally being written in the lives of not only the families within this book, but in the hearts of all who read it. One cannot argue with the testimonies shared in this gripping book; we can only marvel at the truth it reveals in an arena of intensely publically debated values and personal struggles. Enter a world of deep discovery, and be prepared for revelations of the beauty of life, the Creator of life and the insistence of life itself. Be ready to laugh, cry and rethink as you join the amazing journey of ordinary people with extraordinary stories. Embryo adoption has seemed a lofty, philosophically and, sadly, politically untouchable process, but these pages prove that wrong. The solutions to the destiny of these little frozen babies and the history each will have come to life, literally, in the work described within these pages. Maria Lancaster has put feet on her faith and powerfully entered, after personal suffering, with a servant's heart, the very soul of the fight for life in America. You will not regret this read!

Janne Myrdal
North Dakota state director
Concerned Women for America
director@northdakota.cwfa.org

There are many paths that people take to this unique form of adoption, and the journey usually ends with great joy! Maria Lancaster not only was an early participant in embryo adoption, but has gone above and beyond by starting her own embryo adoption program. May the readers of this book be blessed and potentially inspired to explore embryo donation and adoption for themselves!

Kimberly Tyson
Marketing and program director
Embryo Adoption Awareness Center
www.EmbryoAdoption.org

I was inspired by the desire and perseverance of the couples to become parents and their trust in God to guide them on their journey. Many couples will read this book and feel they could write their own chapter. From the generosity of the donor parents to the love of the adoptive parents, I highly recommend *Souls on Ice* to warm the heart.

Rep. Dan Ruby, North Dakota

The names and faces in these stories help explain why the idea that life begins at conception is not just theoretical. Here you get to meet the people for whom it is very, very personal. A very important book.

Joseph Backholm
Executive Director
Family Policy Institute of Washington
www.fpiw.org

Souls On Ice gives us beautiful pictures of the amazing ministry of Embryo Adoption Services of Cedar Park. Their passion for rescuing embryos, and the moving stories of couples struggling with infertility who have had the chance to experience a miracle are inspiring! Maria Lancaster is an amazing and fearless woman who is blessed by invaluable leadership from Dr. Joseph Fuiten, the senior pastor of Cedar Park Church. The Cedar Park commitment to integrity in every detail of the process of each embryo adoption is vital in protecting everyone involved. Maria's vision for bringing families together is inspiring and contagious! I have interviewed several couples that have babies, with Maria, on our radio show, and these shows are some of the most popular we air! You will never see life the same way once you read *Souls on Ice!*

Carrie Abbott
Founder & President, The Legacy Institute
Host of Legacy Out Loud radio show
www.thelegacyinstitute.com

Souls On Ice is a remarkable book that offers infertile couples a new option — embryo adoption. I have been an "adoption" social worker for 23 years. This adoption option is significantly more affordable than traditional types of adoption. The timeframe for being matched (or selected by a genetic donor family) is relatively fast. My clients discover that they are matched with a genetic donor family who is more similar to them than different. This provides a real sense of cohesion and a much easier adoption process than is typical for other types of adoption. There are many other advantages to embryo adoption, including the amazing opportunity for early parent-child bonding/attachment and a healthy womb environment from the start, as well as giving birth. Also, embryo adoption clients and their children seem to value the opportunity to establish contact and even relationships (if desired) with the genetic donor family's children (who are the genetic siblings of the children born through embryo adoption). Nothing really compares to embryo adoption. It is truly a privilege to be a part of this type of adoption. I believe it will grow in popularity as people discover it and become aware of its many advantages.

Heather Basse
MSW, LICSW-WA, LCSW-MO

It was such a pleasure when I spoke at Cedar Park Church in Bothell, Washington, to meet Maria Lancaster, Founder and Executive Director of Embryo Adoption Services of Cedar Park. Maria has a deep passion for her ministry with embryo adoptions. It is amazing that there is a similar connection between her work and what we do in Calcutta, India, as we are both defenders of life. It is wonderful that God has used Maria as an agent to uphold the value of each life. While ministering in Cedar Park Church, it was a great joy for me to meet many families who have benefited from the embryo adoption services and are now happy parents. It is heartwarming that Reverend (Dr.) Joseph Fuiten, the pastor of this church, has included Embryo Adoption Services of Cedar Park with a large number of his other ministries so that families can take advantage of these services.

Reverend (Dr.) Huldah Buntain
President, Assembly of God Mission
Calcutta, India

Astonishing and thought-provoking! Read Maria Lancaster's poignant, often suspenseful account of how the Lancasters' daughter, Elisha, came into their lives after four years in a medical freezer. This and other surreal stories of children adopted as very young embryos — recounted in the first-of-its-kind book, *Souls On Ice* — will forever change your perception of what it means to be a human embryo and may prompt a much needed re-thinking about the pursuit of in vitro fertilization.

Patricia O'Halloran, MD
Internal Medicine Physician

Souls on Ice tells the stories of the heartbreak of infertility, the hope of pregnancy and the heartwarming love of parent for child. This book is a gift to this generation that is yearning to find the morality to keep pace with emerging technology. The stories presented here remind us once again that each human being is unique and unrepeatable. Each has an eternal destiny.

Senator Margaret Sitte
North Dakota

Unique and inspiring. *Souls on Ice* invites you to share some of the most intimate moments in the lives of couples who experienced the miracle of birth through embryo adoption. Like the embryos themselves, each story is unique and reflects God's active role in our lives today.

Ronald L. Stoddart
B.S., J.D. President Emeritus
Nightlight Christian Adoptions

I heartily endorse this book, with its heartwarming and very real collection of personal experiences with embryo adoption. I am a physician researcher and lecturer. I have spent much of the last seven years advocating, explaining, researching and publishing on the subject of embryo adoption. Yet, I can tell you that no scientific information nor facts nor figures can substitute for real human life experiences — that those who have had them are willing to share publicly. Maria Lancaster is both a colleague and a personal friend. I have advocated for Embryo Adoption Services of Cedar Park in many different settings, explaining proudly that Cedar Park is the nation's only *church-based* embryo adoption endeavor. Open this book, and read about these real-life experiences. You will have a new perspective on the beginning of human life.

Reginald Finger, MD, MPH
Assistant Professor
School of Health Sciences
Indiana Wesleyan University

Souls on Ice

True Miracle Stories of Embryo Adoption

New Hope for Infertile Couples

Inspired by the Life and Work of Dr. Maria D. Lancaster

Copyright © 2013 Good Catch Publishing, Beaverton, OR.

All rights reserved. Written permission must be secured from the publisher to use or reproduce any part of this book, except for brief quotations in critical reviews or articles.

This book was written for the express purpose of conveying the love and mercy of Jesus Christ. The statements in this book are substantially true; however, names and minor details have been changed to protect people and situations from accusation or incrimination.

All Scripture quotations, unless otherwise noted, are taken from the New International Version Copyright 1973, 1984, 1987 by International Bible Society.

Published in Beaverton, Oregon, by Good Catch Publishing.
www.goodcatchpublishing.com
V1.1

Printed in the United States of America

Dedication

To all the families who have donated or adopted embryos — and especially to those who have shared their journeys and stories with us. Your courage inspires us every day. We are grateful for your trust and deeply moved by your faith. May God continue to bless you and your wonderful families, for all generations to come.

"Everyone shall stand in awe and confess the greatness of the miracle of God … They will realize what amazing things he does." (Psalm 64:9)

Table of Contents

	Acknowledgements	19
	Foreword	21
	Introduction	27
1	Child of Destiny	29
2	Waiting	85
3	The Answer	105
4	Hope Rests	121
5	Babies Everywhere!	149
6	Surprise Blessings	167
7	The Giving	187
8	The Heart of a Miracle	193
9	Hypothetical Utopia	227
10	Miracles, a Country Apart	257
11	Our Gift	271
12	The Life Spark	289
	Conclusion	305
	What Other Families Are Saying…	309
	Resources	327

Acknowledgements

I would first like to thank my husband and daughter, Jeff and Elisha, for allowing me the time and energy away from them in order to organize and compile this collection of amazing miracle stories. Elisha, you are my inspiration, and Jeff, you are my anchor.

I would also like to thank our Co-founder, Dr. Joseph Fuiten, for his vision for this ministry and this book. No one could ask for a better friend, mentor or pastor. Your leadership paved the way for every born baby.

Thank you to my prayer partners who have prayed this book through from the very beginning, Peggy and Walt Johnson, Katherine and Phil Cassady, George and Friedel Votava, Drs. Greg and Cyndi Romine, Debi Fry, Betty Heidi and countless others too numerous to list.

It is impossible to adequately acknowledge the storytellers in this book. You have helped create a great gift to others — a gift of hope, faith and great love. Thank you and God bless you for your willingness to be so vulnerable, waiting on the Lord for your victory and sharing it with the world.

Thanks and appreciation to all of the great leaders who sent their endorsements for this book. Your affirmation and support will help spread the "Good News." Also, every one of our families that sent a "Word of Encouragement," thank you for your inspiration and love.

Souls on Ice

A very special "thank you" to Governor Mike Huckabee. You touched our hearts with your love, kindness and generosity. Your comprehension of the true value of human life, even an embryo, is changing the culture and society through your words and deeds.

This book would not have been published without the amazing efforts of Good Catch Publishing's Project Manager and Editor, Hayley Pandolph. Her untiring resolve pushed this project forward and turned it into a stunning victory. Thank you for your great fortitude and diligence. Deep thanks to incredible Editor in Chief, Michelle Cuthrell, and Executive Editor, Jen Genovesi, for all the amazing work they do. I would also like to thank Good Catch's invaluable Proofreader, Melody Davis, for the focus and energy she has put into perfecting our words.

Lastly, I want to extend our gratitude to the creative and very talented Jenny Randle, who designed the exceptionally beautiful cover for *Souls on Ice: True Miracle Stories of Embryo Adoption.*

Dr. Maria D. Lancaster
Co-Founder and Executive Director
Embryo Adoption Services of Cedar Park

Foreword

Life begins at conception — not some arbitrary point thereafter, but at the very moment of conception. Every embryo is a human life, unique and individual, with worth and value, and absolutely deserving of protection by society.

I became even more convinced of this truth when I met Maria Lancaster in 2007. I was running for president when she approached me on the campaign trail in Bellevue, Washington, and handed me a photograph of her daughter, Elisha.

Elisha came to her parents through embryo adoption. A surplus embryo from another couple's fertility treatment, she was frozen for four years at just two cells. In 2003, she was taken out of the freezer and placed inside Maria's womb. When Elisha was born, she was the 36th child in the world to be born in such a fashion.

When I heard Elisha's story, I knew that science had once again made strides toward affirming that life begins *at conception.*

I thanked Maria and tucked the snapshot she gave me in my wallet. I couldn't quit thinking about this little girl who represented such a clear picture that life is valuable. Elisha lives a full life and is loved by her parents. And I couldn't help but wonder, *What would have happened if Jeff and Maria Lancaster had not considered and valued the fact that an embryo is a human life?* She could have been a medical experiment or discarded as medical waste.

During ABC's *Nightline* program later in the campaign, an interviewer asked me, "What do you have in your wallet?" I pulled out Elisha's picture and briefly told the story.

I still carry her picture in my wallet today. I have kept it there for six years. When people ask me why I am pro-life, I open my wallet, bring out the photo and show them a living reason. I have to ask them, "Would you be willing to tell the mother of this child that her child wasn't worth saving?"

Human embryo adoption gives us an opportunity to honor tiny lives that hang in the balance — and in the freezer.

Elisha is a true gift from God, born through the miracle of embryo adoption. Hearing her story and meeting her, as I did during another trip to Washington State, has given me a deep and remarkably personal understanding of what life really means.

I think that, as a society, we've created the illusion that an embryo is just a blob of tissue and not a human being. People often suggest that it doesn't matter if we experiment with frozen embryos because they are not really alive. Let me be clear: Elisha is a real person. She is not just tissue. She is not fodder for medical experimentation. She is a loving little girl with a powerful story. And she, and others like her, are worth saving.

Meeting Maria Lancaster was a life-changing

Foreword

experience for me. Since 2007, she has partnered with Cedar Park Church's pastor, Dr. Joseph B. Fuiten, to found Embryo Adoption Services of Cedar Park and is helping other people discover embryo adoption as an option when they're struggling to have children. I've come to learn that one in four couples suffers with infertility, while in America nearly a million frozen embryos wait for their chance at life. Embryo adoption is real new hope for infertile couples.

Maria works relentlessly to protect the lives of the unborn. Her efforts to connect families who have remaining embryos after fertility treatments with those who are unable to conceive are incredible. God orchestrates every match in her organization, and the power of his direction in the process is reflected in this new compilation of true stories.

It is my hope that this book will impact you in a positive and meaningful way. I hope the stories touch you, change you and make you think twice about when life begins.

I told Maria that I would work diligently to protect human life, whatever form it takes. I now ask you to do the same.

May these stories cause you to stand in awe of our great God, who knows us deeply long before we are born. He is, after all, the precious author and giver of the gift of life.

Mike Huckabee

The book you are about to read
is a compilation of authentic life stories.
The facts are true, and the events are real.
These storytellers have dealt with crisis and tragedy
and have shared their most private moments, mess-ups
and hang-ups in order for others to learn and grow from
them. In order to protect the identities of those involved
in their pasts, the names and details of some storytellers
have been withheld or changed.

Introduction

We offer this book to you as a sign of hope.

Hope for couples who desire to have a child, but so far cannot. Hope for families who wonder *what next* for embryos remaining from their fertility treatments.

And hope for anyone who wonders whether there really is a living and a loving God — one who notices us and who cares about the very details of our lives, our dreams and our heartaches.

The stories in this book are true. The families interviewed are real. Some have donated embryos. Others adopted them. There are biracial families, Asian and Hispanic families, African-American families and some from other countries. Some parents are older, some relatively young. Some families pursued open adoption, some did not.

They have one thing in common: embryo donation and embryo adoption and the marvelous way the sharing of a few small cells changed their lives forever.

You will read the intimate details of their lives — their medical and financial frustrations, their bewilderment, pain, sorrow and disappointment and also their profound joy and thankfulness.

Each story is unique. Each reveals how God heard and answered their cries, in mysterious and amazing ways. How each family became matched at *just the right time*

Souls on Ice

offers wondrous evidence not of coincidence, but of God's fingerprints on our lives.

Medical advances in fertility treatments certainly created ethical dilemmas regarding what to do with remaining embryos. Embryo adoption offers a new hope and a new option, one which is affordable, accessible and available.

In addition to firsthand accounts by families who have either donated or adopted embryos, this book will provide you with practical information about what to do, how to proceed and who to contact if *you* are interested in embryo donation or adoption.

There IS a loving God in our midst. I hope and pray this book touches you and gives you hope. May you find a new or renewed awareness that God loves you and cares about even the smallest details of *your* life.

Feel free to contact us for more information. We'd love to hear from you!

Dr. Joseph B. Fuiten
Senior Pastor, Cedar Park Church
www.cedarpark.org
Co-Founder, President
Embryo Adoption Services
of Cedar Park
www.AdoptEmbryos.org
www.DonateEmbryos.org
1-888-959-7712

Child of Destiny
The Adoption Story of Jeff and Maria Lancaster
Written by Joy Steiner Moore

My mind was a flurry of overwhelming thoughts as the White House staffer ushered us ceremoniously into the historic East Room, past the rows of legislators, lobbyists and sea of members of the media. She directed each of us ladies to our seats on the platform, instructing our husbands to stand directly behind us.

I glanced back nervously at my husband, Jeff, who was holding our 2-year-old daughter, Elisha, dressed in a pink satin dress with a matching bow in her hair. The other mothers and fathers held their small children, too, and I felt the camaraderie among us. Our families were honored to have flown across the country to be on the stage supporting President Bush as he discussed his veto of the funding of embryonic stem cell research, and we could only hope that our toddlers wouldn't make a scene during his half-hour live, nationally televised speech.

Elisha drank in her surroundings with her big hazel eyes and seemed remarkably calm, considering the events of the busy afternoon had left no time for her nap. Jeff kissed Elisha's forehead and smiled back at me. He rested a hand on my shoulder, putting me at ease in a way only he knew how.

Souls on Ice

I turned my attention back to the doorway, where it looked like things were about to begin. A knot formed in my stomach, and I reached up a trembling hand to smooth my hair.

"Ladies and gentlemen, the President of the United States!"

We stood to our feet, applauding the entrance of President George W. Bush. He moved quickly and purposefully down the aisle and onto the stage, greeting us all warmly.

"Hi, everybody," he said easily, smiling and meeting the eyes of those of us closest to him. "Please be seated."

He turned around to face the audience and grabbed the podium firmly with both hands.

"Good afternoon. Congress has just passed and sent to my desk two bills concerning the use of embryonic stem cells in biomedical research … In this new era, our challenge is to harness the power of science to ease human suffering without sanctioning the practices that violate the dignity of human life."

We applauded. The president waited, and I noticed how he shuffled his feet restlessly behind the podium. *Even the president gets nervous,* I thought. It made me feel better.

The reality of where we were began to sink in.

He's so close. If I stick my toe out, I could touch the president's shoe.

He continued his speech, explaining how the first bill would fund stem cell research. The speech was punctuated

Child of Destiny

only by the squeals and chatter of the young children behind him — "snowflake babies," as they were called. They started out as frozen embryos remaining from the in vitro fertilization process, and if not for being adopted and given a womb to grow in, would never have been given the chance to share their squeals and chatter with the world. The irony of that fact was not lost on me.

"Congress has also passed a second bill ... This bill would support the taking of innocent human life in the hope of finding medical benefits for others. It crosses a moral boundary that our decent society needs to respect, so I vetoed it."

The room erupted into hearty applause, cheers and enthusiastic whistles of approval. Everyone stood, united in praise for the president's decision. But those of us on the platform clapped the hardest and loudest. We were united as pioneers in embryo adoption, my own daughter being the 36th in the world and the first one born in Washington State.

Right then, as I sat with my husband and daughter in the East Room of the White House, just inches from the President of the United States, I believed that this moment was the beginning of the rest of my life. I had no idea of what was to come, but I instinctively knew that we were on a new path.

I was suddenly overwhelmed by my passion for these unborn babies. The enormity of the situation struck me hard as I realized how many thousands and thousands of embryos were still on ice, waiting for the chance to be

Souls on Ice

born. It was an issue not many people were aware of, and I knew that I needed to do *more*.

This most certainly is going to change everything.

❧❧❧

I was 32 years old when I met Jeff Lancaster. He was the solid, friendly and effervescent counterpart to my outspoken, activist nature, and I loved him deeply. But I think what I loved the most was his unwavering relationship with God and committed Christian faith. I knew he was the right one for me. We married a few years after we met and eventually settled on a horse ranch in Snoqualmie, Washington, at the foothills of the Cascade Mountains, not far from Seattle.

Jeff had two young sons from a previous marriage, and I threw myself into helping to raise them — I was a stepmom, cooking, driving and helping in every area I could. I had responsibility but lacked authority, which was a frustrating combination for me as a stepparent. We also raised my niece from the age of 10, making us another modern blended family. My niece was such a joy to me and really inspired me to have a baby of my own. But I couldn't imagine bringing one more child into the exceedingly busy situation. In addition to our family responsibilities, we each had our own businesses to run — Jeff's general contracting business and my shipping supply company, which served the Alaskan fishing fleet with groceries and supplies. Even when we weren't working, we were busy all the time with family activities and responsibilities.

When we finally got around to seriously trying for a baby, I was 37, which is considered "old" as far as the medical community is concerned. It took us a couple of years, but we finally got pregnant naturally. We announced to all of our friends and family the joyful news that we were expecting a baby at last!

But our happiness was short-lived. About three months into the pregnancy, I miscarried. We knew that it was rare to miscarry after the first trimester, so we were understandably shocked. The doctor called it a blighted ovum.

The loss was extremely painful for me, both physically and emotionally. I was embarrassed, having made the big announcement to my family and friends. I was so disappointed, and my heart sank.

Like many other couples, however, we wanted to try again. Nearly one in four couples struggles with infertility, but no one likes to talk about it. I had heard about an amazing church in Bothell, Washington, that, on the last Sunday in January each year, prayed specifically for couples struggling with infertility. A lot of ladies — in fact, hundreds over the years — had ended up getting pregnant after they were prayed for, so there was some buzz going around about the success of "Presentation Sunday," as they called it. They had even been on the local news. The pastor, Joe Fuiten, encouraged couples to tell the amazing stories of what God had done in their lives. Knowing about our struggles, our own local pastor encouraged us to go.

What can it hurt? I thought to myself.

So on the last Sunday in January that year, Jeff and I drove to Cedar Park Church. We went into the large, open sanctuary and sat down. I could feel the sweet presence of the Lord. As the service began, I felt no hope, and I wondered why I had even come. I started to feel so uncomfortable that I suggested to Jeff that we leave. We listened to the pastor's sermon, and as we sat in the pew, I chided myself for being so cynical and unbelieving that God could actually heal my body and help me get pregnant again. But when it was time for prayer, we went forward, anyway. I was touched by the sheer number of couples at the altar, dozens and dozens of families, filling the front of the church. Pastor Fuiten prayed for us that day, and I returned home feeling extremely hopeful. *God is changing my heart,* I thought.

Time marched on, and at 43 another miracle pregnancy occurred. My heart soared, and I thought that our promised child was on the way. But sadly, a few months later, that pregnancy also ended in a very painful miscarriage.

The rollercoaster of emotions was exhausting. It was wearying for our hopes to be lifted so high and then to be dashed so completely. It reminded me of the scripture in the Bible that reads, "Hope deferred makes the heart sick, but a longing fulfilled is a tree of life" (Proverbs 13:12). Where was my "tree of life"? I was out of answers, but I trusted that God had a plan. We were on the right path. I could feel it in my gut.

I knew I was called to be a mother. Raising Jeff's sons and my niece had brought that part of me to life, and we now wanted our own baby so badly. Our family had so much love to give. But in my heart, I began to wonder if it was ever going to be a reality for us. I knew I was going to have to trust God completely — that his plan was good and his timing was perfect.

❧❧❧

Even traditional adoption seemed unrealistic. I was 46, and we were too old to be seriously considered for adoption, and even if we were approved, we couldn't afford the many thousands it would cost. We weren't interested in foster care. I did not feel called to take on a temporary or uncertain role. Though I had already helped raise three kids, I found that I never had true parental authority. I wanted to raise a child with my husband, and it looked like we were running out of options.

We were attending a great church at the time, and one weekend, an evangelist named Emmanuel Ziga came to preach. He was a captivating speaker, and at the end of the sermon, Dr. Ziga stood silently on the platform, as if listening quietly to what God wanted to say to him.

"I believe there is somebody here who desires to have a child," he said at last, each word accentuated by his heavy African accent.

Souls on Ice

I immediately knew in my heart that he was talking about me. I broke out in an instant sweat. I exchanged knowing glances with Jeff and then moved quickly to the end of my row and made my way to the front of the church. Dr. Ziga saw me coming and met me at the altar.

"Open this womb," he prayed, laying his hands firmly on my shoulders. "Fill this womb. Child of destiny!"

At those last words, chills flooded my body. I returned to my seat and wrote down every word he'd prayed so that I would never forget them. *Child of destiny.* The prayer was so impactful and encouraging that it restored my hope and joy. I felt like it was a promise from God himself. In the days and weeks that followed, I read and re-read it, again and again. *Our child is on the way!*

Within weeks, I took a pregnancy test, and for the third time in my life, it was *positive.* My mouth hung open as I stared at the test in my hand. I absolutely could not believe it.

Jeff and I rejoiced. We were thrilled!

This is the child of promise! This is the child God has sent us! Child of destiny!

We had long since decided on a name for our baby, and Jeff printed it off the computer and posted it on the refrigerator in our kitchen: Elisha (meaning "God is my salvation") Ramiah (meaning "Yahweh shall be exalted"). Every time we went to the fridge, we were reminded of God's promise to us, and we praised him for his extreme goodness. We went on with life, planning a nursery and telling our friends and family.

Child of Destiny

But then, it happened again. The all-too-familiar cramping and spotting began, followed by the rush to the doctor's office and an ultrasound picture devoid of all signs of life. I suffered yet another miscarriage.

I almost let myself sink into despair.

God, why are you doing this to me? Why even let me get pregnant if it's not meant to be? How will I ever recover from this?

There are not words to describe my disappointment. I was 46 years old and felt like my last shot at motherhood had just been taken away. Everywhere I went I saw happy mothers with babies. It made me feel physically ill to think that I would never be able to hold my babies. Some days I wanted to curl up into a fetal position and never get up again.

But I knew that if I let myself succumb to that negative state of mind, I would certainly lose the will to live. If I were to survive this crushing blow, I needed to do something *opposite* of what I really *wanted* to do, so I gave myself a little talk:

I know God spoke to me. I know he told me that there's a child on the way. This situation is so completely beyond me that only God can redeem this situation now. So I can either believe what he said or not.

I prayed that God would give me courage to pursue the idea he had planted in me. I knew that we had a "child of destiny." I decided to defy what was happening to me and respond by believing in what God had promised. I drove to a secondhand shop, The Lost Mitten, in North

Souls on Ice

Bend. They specialized in supplies for babies. I found myself standing outside the plate-glass window, admiring the high chairs, baby toys and soft blankets on display. My heart yearned for all of it, but it was the beautiful white cradle right in front that caught my eye. I stood on the sidewalk imagining that cradle at the foot of our bed ... I envisioned soft lullabies and a sweet baby's contented sleep. I knew that I was supposed to buy that cradle.

When I got home, I placed the cradle at the end of our bed.

"Somehow, I don't know how, but that crib will be full," I said to Jeff that evening.

"Okay," he said. "We'll just trust God and see what happens."

I didn't go back to the doctor, and I stopped researching avenues for adoption. I did absolutely nothing. Jeff and I went back to living our lives, trusting that in God's perfect timing, he would fill the little white cradle with the child he had promised us. All we could do was wait. It seemed totally opposite of what a normal person would do that was trying to have a baby. The key, I realize in hindsight, was that I surrendered.

ಞಞಞ

Dinner was almost ready, and I bustled busily about my kitchen, setting the table and tossing together a salad. I heard the rumble of Jeff's blue Ford contractor pickup truck as he pulled up the gravel road on our farm. I could tell from the sound of his truck door slamming shut and his quick footsteps that he was in a hurry. I turned around from the fridge just as he entered the kitchen and placed his hands on the counter. *Wow,* I thought. *Something big must have happened today.*

"Maria." His eyes were alive with excitement.

"What? What is it?"

"I was just listening to Dr. Dobson on the radio."

I raised an eyebrow with interest. We both loved Dr. James Dobson and his Focus on the Family ministry, but Dr. Dobson's radio program was hard to catch out on the farm with our poor radio reception. Luckily, he was able to listen to the show while driving.

"He was interviewing a woman named Marlene," Jeff continued. "You know how when couples do in vitro fertilization, there are remaining embryos that do not get transferred for a pregnancy? The embryos are frozen until the couple decides what to do with them. Well, Marlene Strege and her husband were the first couple to *adopt* a frozen embryo. She had the embryo transferred into her uterus, and she got pregnant, and now she and her husband have a daughter named Hannah!"

Jeff paused and looked me right in the eyes.

"Maria, that is *exactly* what you're supposed to do."

I felt like the room was beginning to spin. I was lightheaded from the few moments where I forgot to breathe.

Is this our answer?

It honestly sounded a little crazy.

Souls on Ice

Carry someone else's baby?

And yet, I completely believed that remaining embryos were people — human life. They deserved a chance to be born. We talked about it for hours.

The next day, I picked up the phone and called Focus on the Family's headquarters. I asked what agency Marlene and her husband had gone through for their embryo adoption, and they gave me a phone number for Nightlight Christian Adoptions in California. I called the agency the very next day. They called the babies "Snowflakes" — each one unique, yet frozen.

The course of our lives was about to change.

❧❧❧

Over the next few weeks, I researched as much about embryo adoption as I possibly could. I learned that there were only four options for couples with remaining embryos in cryopreservation after fertility treatments were complete: They could keep freezing them indefinitely, they could donate them for embryonic stem cell research, they could legally throw them away or they could make them available to another family. Embryo donation seemed, to me, like the right thing to do.

The very thought that there was a choice between throwing away an embryo or giving it a chance to be born was shocking to me. If that same embryo were placed in a woman's womb, it would grow into a baby, so how was discarding it even an option? It seemed to me that

Child of Destiny

throwing away or donating an embryo to scientific research was a tragic end to a human life.

How could anybody throw away a life?

And yet, it seemed that thousands of couples faced this dilemma throughout the world. In 2003, there were approximately 400,000 embryos currently being frozen, or cryopreserved, awaiting a decision as to their fate.

As far as an alternative to fertility treatments, I liked the idea of embryo adoption because there were already plenty of embryos available in cryopreservation. Adopting couples were merely giving existing embryos a chance at life. But I could only imagine the dilemma donating families faced when told that their donated embryos would be given to a "good, stable and loving family." How could they know if their child would be raised with the same values? Would it be better to leave the embryos frozen rather than send it to some random people to raise? I could see the potential for terrible dilemmas for families with remaining embryos in the freezer.

Nightlight provided a Christian environment for donating couples to be carefully matched with prescreened adopting families.

I knew that Jeff was right. This was the path that we were supposed to pursue. At that time, only 10 babies in the United States had been born from donated frozen embryos, and I somehow knew that it was exactly the path that God was calling us to.

I made a doctor's appointment with a fertility specialist to make sure that my body was still healthy enough for pregnancy. I also needed to pinpoint why I had miscarried in the past, and after considerable research, I believed it may be due to a condition called Antiphospholipid Syndrome. The syndrome is an immune system problem that causes a woman's body to perceive the embryo as an invader. It was treatable if diagnosed. I told my doctor I wanted blood work done and sent to a special lab in California for testing. After a bit of coercing, he finally agreed. My diagnosis was confirmed, just as I had suspected, and I began to take the recommended treatments, aspirin and heparin.

I had to have a complete physical, despite my clean bill of health. I was 47, and I was an older candidate for the adoption agency, and I worried that I might never get matched with a donor family. It took a few months, and a few moments of nearly giving up, before we were finally matched with a family in North Carolina. I was amazed at their similarities to us on paper. They were older and self-employed, as were we. They were also of German and English descent, and photos of the young men in the family actually resembled my brothers. But the best thing of all was that they, too, were Christians and attended a church similar to ours. Though we never met the couple or spoke with them, we learned all about them through a family profile with pictures, letters and thorough medical histories provided by Nightlight.

At some point, as the adoption process began to move forward, I had a few moments where I wondered if we were doing the right thing. There were so many unknowns. I confided in two different friends, and neither of them responded positively. In fact, I was certain they thought we were completely nuts.

"I think I've finally realized there is no way we can talk to anybody about this," I told Jeff one evening. "Everybody thinks we're grasping desperately at straws. They will discourage it, so why bother?"

Jeff and I decided right then that we would keep it to ourselves. It was a private matter, and nobody needed to know about it. After mulling it over, I couldn't imagine a situation where someone would take note of our future child and ask, "Oh, by the way, how did that happen?"

Even if I became pregnant and we had a baby, nobody necessarily needed to know where the baby came from. "No one asks you that, in the real world," I chuckled.

In the meantime, I was praying a lot. There's a story in the Bible about a man named Abraham, and he and his wife, Sarah, could not have children. Even after God appeared to him and promised him that he and Sarah would have a son, Abraham took matters into his own hands. He slept with Sarah's maid, Hagar, and had a son named Ishmael. Several years later, Sarah did give birth to Isaac, the son God had promised. Abraham's impatience and Ishmael's resulting existence caused a lot of strife in their family and among his descendants for thousands of years, even into today. *If God has spoken to me,* I thought, *I shouldn't try to get ahead and have this baby through my own reasoning and strength.*

As I pursued embryo adoption, I was mindful that I

did not want to be orchestrating an Ishmael experience. I knew that if we made a mistake that we would have to live with it for the rest of our lives. I needed to make sure that I was hearing directly from God and not trying to force a pregnancy and child into existence. I asked God to show me some undeniable confirmation that by adopting an embryo we were doing the right thing.

❦❦❦

In the fall of 2002, Jeff and I served on a mission trip to Italy, with our ministry friends, Drs. Greg and Cyndi Romine. When we left the States, the adoption papers had not yet been signed, and there seemed to be a lot of details still up in the air. It was difficult not to be anxious about it, but I kept praying that if the embryo adoption was meant to be, God would work out all the details and make it clear to us one way or another.

A sweet 90-year-old Italian lady named Aunt Emma in the church we were visiting prayed for me after I shared with her my desire to have a baby, and I felt a wonderful sense of peace overwhelm me and calm my heart as she prayed. My preoccupation with the topic disappeared, and I was able to enjoy the remainder of the trip without worry. We had a wonderful time with our friends, made new Italian friends, had wonderful Christian fellowship and ate a lot of outstanding Italian food. It was like a vacation on top of a mission trip.

Child of Destiny

We arrived home, feeling the weight of uncertainty about whether or not our adoption was going to finalize. The following Sunday, we attended church. As the worship service began, I noticed one of the worship leaders looking panicked. His head turned from side to side, as if he couldn't find something he was looking for. *What is wrong with him?* I thought.

Suddenly, he set his microphone on the carpet and marched down the aisle and up to the balcony where we were sitting. He stopped right in front of us.

"Contracts are being signed!" he announced with force, as if delivering an important message. He then turned around and walked back to the front of the church.

My mouth dropped open, and I just about fell out of my seat. Nobody in our church knew what we were planning. It was, without a doubt, I felt, a message from God. After that, I was a weeping ball of tears. Several days later, we learned that indeed the next portion of paperwork had been completed. Our embryo transfer date, January 28, 2003, was looking more and more like a reality.

☙☙☙

The same friends who had gone with us on the mission trip, Drs. Greg and Cyndi, wanted Jeff to do a remodel on their kitchen. I tagged along with him to Vancouver for the weekend. Even though the Romines were great friends and mentors, we still didn't feel

Souls on Ice

comfortable sharing our adoption plans with them just yet. *Let's just see if this works out. Maybe I won't even have anything to explain.*

At the end of the weekend, when the remodel was complete, Cyndi handed me an envelope. I waited until we had driven away before I tore it open and slid out a greeting card displaying a lovely print from Anne Geddes — a baby girl's face surrounded by purple hydrangeas. I opened the card.

Thank you for the beautiful kitchen, the note read in Cyndi's lovely handwriting. *By the way, she's on her way.*

My heart skipped a beat. I dropped the card in my lap.

She's on her way ... does she mean our baby? How did she know?

"What does it say?" Jeff asked without taking his eyes off the road.

I was silent for a long moment, drinking in the landscape outside my window — rolling farmland interspersed with tall trees, a hallmark of the Pacific Northwest. God's creation was breathtaking, and it spoke of his great majesty. He saw to so many details, and it was extremely humbling to realize that he would love me so much as to care for my details, too.

How good God is to show us we are doing the right thing.

Jeff cast me a sideways glance. He was still waiting for an answer.

"Our baby's on her way," I choked out, my voice hardly more than a whisper.

Child of Destiny

That night, we settled into our hotel room near Vancouver and turned on the TV to watch a Christmas special. I was exhausted. Cyndi's card was wonderful and emotionally overwhelming. *How had she known?*

As we flipped through the channels, we finally settled on *It's a Wonderful Life*. I had seen it many times before, but this time, with the embryo transfer scheduled just a little more than a month away, it seemed more like a good distraction to keep my mind off of the anxiety that kept trying to creep in.

I watched for the umpteenth time as George Bailey, Jimmy Stewart's character, endured a series of financial misfortunes leading him to stagger toward a bridge with the intention of committing suicide. Things had gotten so bad for him that he believed he never should have been born. But Clarence the guardian angel came to George's rescue and began showing him what the town would have been like had he not ever existed. As it turned out, the world was a pretty sad place without George in it.

I suddenly sat up on the edge of the bed. The revelation was as clear as day. If I didn't go through with this adoption, this child would never be born. If the child wasn't born, *history would literally be changed*, just like George's existence and life changed history in the movie.

It became crystal clear to me. I couldn't let the unknowns dictate my feelings. There was nothing more important than this little embryo and the chance Jeff and I were giving it to be a living, breathing person in the world. Who was I to prevent this child from his or her destiny?

Souls on Ice

No longer was this about *my* desire for a baby. This was suddenly about this child's right to live and the plan God had for his or her life.

Almost 2,900 miles away, in North Carolina, tiny frozen embryos were being prepared to embark on a FedEx journey across the country. Having been frozen at -200 degrees for four years, these little ones, made up of two cells, were finally being given their chance. And Jeff and I were finally ready — emotionally, physically and spiritually.

❧❧❧

No embryo adoptions had ever taken place in the State of Washington, and ours was slated to be the first. We appreciated my fertility doctor for being so willing to take part in such a pioneering movement.

Our embryos arrived at Dr. Kevin Johnson's office in Bellevue, Washington, via FedEx. They were carefully stored cryogenically at -200 degrees. On the day of the transfer, they would have to go through a thawing process. In the meantime, I took the necessary hormone shots to prepare my womb for the embryo transfer. I was also continuing to take heparin and aspirin so that if I got pregnant with the embryos, my body would not reject them. The plan was to transfer two embryos from the donor family at one time.

On the morning of the transfer, we met with Dr. Johnson at the fertility clinic.

Child of Destiny

"Would you like to see the embryos?" he asked, sitting back in his chair and casually cleaning his glasses.

My eyes widened.

"Could we?"

Dr. Johnson nodded and led us to another room where a microscope and a monitor were set up. He directed us to the monitor, where we could actually see what was under the microscope in the adjacent laboratory. We anxiously waited for the embryos to come into focus.

"Here you go. Look here. They are about eight cells now." He smiled.

Jeff and I looked at the screen, awestruck at the miracle in progress. The embryos looked like glass, shiny and translucent. *How does God make a baby, a placenta and an umbilical cord from that?* I thought. Hope surged in my heart for them, and I let out a long, ragged breath of emotion. This day had been a long time coming, and the moment of truth had arrived. The embryos had survived the thaw. I was shaking, I was so overwhelmed.

I turned around from the monitor and faced Jeff and Dr. Johnson.

"I'm ready now, if you are, to transfer the embryos," I said, attempting a brave smile.

Dr. Johnson nodded reassuringly and prepared the rest of his medical team for the embryo transfer.

☙☙☙

Souls on Ice

The doctor transferred both embryos into my uterus, and the waiting game began. It was the longest 10 days of my life. One of the most difficult things was not telling anyone. Here, we had just gone through this very emotional process making this huge decision, and now we were attempting to just live our lives, acting as if nothing out of the ordinary was going on.

Then, a pregnancy test revealed the big news: The transfer was successful, and I was pregnant! The home pregnancy test was confirmed when we went into the clinic for a blood test. I was shocked and overwhelmed and happy. I was also so tired I thought I could sleep for a week. Years of loss and pain melted away as dreams of holding our baby filled my mind and soul.

Despite their willingness and enthusiasm to go through with the embryo transfer procedure, Dr. Johnson and his staff were absolutely shocked to hear the good report. After all, I was 47 at the time!

Jeff and I were just grateful to God. We knew that he alone was the author of life, and we felt privileged to be a part of the process. It was such a miracle that after being frozen in suspended animation at two cells for four years, an embryo could be thawed and planted in a womb, and life would begin to grow again, just as it would have naturally.

Child of Destiny

When I was eight weeks pregnant, life was humming right along, and I drove down to Portland to attend a women's conference. During a lunch break on the last day of the conference, I leaned under a table to pick up a package of cups so I could pour myself a drink. As I stood back up, I felt something *happen*, almost like something had ruptured. My heart sank.

Oh, no. Not again.

Very slowly and carefully, I placed the cups on the table and walked gingerly to the nearest restroom, avoiding eye contact with everyone I passed.

Safely in the ladies' room, I found refuge in a stall. The sheer amount of blood I saw was absolutely horrifying. I had seen this kind of thing before, and I knew for sure that I was having a miscarriage.

I felt numb as I gathered my luggage from the hotel and began the long drive back to Seattle.

This can't be real. God, why?

I drove the three-hour trip home in the dark and in a torrential downpour. I felt as chilled on the inside as it was outside. Somehow, I made it back home. Jeff and I prayed together that night that somehow our embryos had survived. First thing the next morning, I picked up the phone and called my doctor's office.

"I think I'm having a miscarriage," I told the nurse, swallowing a lump in my throat.

"Oh, Maria." The nurse, Jo, was sympathetic. "Have you had any cramping?"

"Well … no." I hesitated. "Just a lot of bleeding."

Souls on Ice

"Why don't you come on in and have the doctor do an ultrasound? Don't worry just yet. Let's see what he says first." A ray of hope filtered in through the sadness.

In the ultrasound room, we were on pins and needles and preparing ourselves for the worst. If it really was a miscarriage, I didn't know how I was going to face it.

But suddenly, through the machine's speakers, the comforting sound of a fast little heartbeat filled the room. Dr. Johnson grinned with relief, and Jo stood nearby, beaming.

"Is that …?" My eyes filled with tears of joy.

"Yes, Maria. The baby looks and sounds good." The doctor pointed to the little peanut on the screen. "But I do think that maybe what you experienced was the loss of this baby's twin."

Twin? I stared at him in disbelief.

"That's what it looks like to me. But this baby still looks really good. Just take it easy, okay?"

We grieved for the life of one child and took comfort knowing that our baby was with the Lord. At the same time, we thanked God for the precious little one whose heart was still beating.

☙☙☙

It was easy to "take it easy," because for the next few months, I was dreadfully ill. The only relief I found was in sleep. I couldn't work or load the dishwasher or even sleep in my own bed. I was completely miserable. I had off-the-wall cravings, like cottage cheese with honey or scrambled eggs with ketchup. Sometimes in the afternoon I would sneak out and go to the nearest Mexican restaurant because I just had to have nachos — and I don't even like nachos.

But even with the extreme sickness and other usual pregnancy complaints, I was really just so grateful for the miracle growing inside me. Again and again, as I lay on the sofa feeling like death itself, I quoted scriptures from the Bible to remind myself of God's goodness. Psalm 139 was one of my favorites:

"For you created my inmost being; you knit me together in my mother's womb. I praise you because I am fearfully and wonderfully made; your works are wonderful, I know that full well. My frame was not hidden from you when I was made in the secret place, when I was woven together in the depths of the earth. Your eyes saw my unformed body; all the days ordained for me were written in your book before one of them came to be."

I marveled at those beautiful words.

In my fifth month, I finally started feeling like a person again. My brother, Michael, called and asked if I would take his daughter, Rachel, horseback riding. We all walked out on the trails with the horses and had a great day. As I walked along, I marveled that he did not notice I was five months pregnant. We had decided it was too soon to tell the family, so we waited some more.

We didn't want to tell our families our news until I knew that even if I went into premature labor, the baby had a good chance of surviving. We had been through so many losses that I knew my family was tired of the rollercoaster ride as well.

I also knew that my age would be a concern and would cause them anxiety and fear. I was leery of my announcement putting them on the spot for a positive reaction. It had to be handled delicately so they would have a chance to process the information.

In the meantime, I had been wondering about the baby's gender. While I knew that I would love whoever God chose to give us, I secretly hoped for a girl. I just didn't know if I was ready for the busy-ness of a little boy at my age. I also knew that God had given me the name Elisha. I trusted that his plan was better than mine, and we awaited the gender reveal.

When the day came to find out, I made small talk with Dr. Elisabeth Evans as she rubbed the ultrasound gel over my rounded abdomen. I tried to keep my mind off of the fact that in just a few minutes the entire path of my motherhood journey would be determined.

"Well," she said at last, "I don't see what's supposed to be here if it's a boy. So I think it's a girl."

In that one statement, my mind was put at ease. The name God had given us was going to be used! I couldn't wait to tell Jeff. We were going to have a daughter!

A girl!

We felt it was safe to tell our families. On Mother's Day in 2003, we sent out a letter announcing our new addition coming in October, and we included an ultrasound picture of the baby with her hand waving. We did not share *how* we got pregnant. We felt the pregnancy itself was enough.

It took a couple of days before the congratulations began rolling in. Like I thought, our family members needed time to process the information, and our chosen method of communication gave them that. They were all thrilled!

☙☙☙

As she grew inside me, our baby girl used my uterus as a trampoline. She was constantly active, often waking me up as early as 4 a.m. with her jumping act. It was so distracting, it was impossible to even think about sleeping.

But when I was 32 weeks pregnant, I awoke on a September morning to an eerie stillness. I looked at the alarm clock and was surprised to see that it was almost 7 a.m. She'd let me sleep in for once, and that was unusual. I lay in bed massaging my stomach, trying to stimulate the baby's activity. But there was no movement. Not wanting to wake up Jeff, I began to silently panic.

What if she's dead?

I stared at the ceiling above our bed and visualized our baby girl's funeral — a white tent at the cemetery with a tiny white casket and tons of late-summer flowers scattered on the top. And Jeff and myself, crushed.

Stop it, Maria, I told myself, shaking my head as if I

could simply shake off the negative thoughts. I sat up on the side of the bed.

Sugar. Maybe sugar would help wake her up.

I padded out to the kitchen and poured myself some orange juice. *Come on, baby girl. Move.*

When the orange juice didn't help, I ate some Cheerios. I felt the slightest little movement then, but I wasn't going to wait around for more. I knew in my heart that something was wrong. I casually got dressed so as not to alarm Jeff. I remained as calm as I could on the outside because I knew that if he flipped out, I couldn't keep him together, too. It was all I could do to rein in my own emotions.

I climbed into my car and drove to the hospital alone. It was the only way I could cope.

I parked at a convenient spot, not caring if they towed my car away. As soon as I got in a room and on a gurney, they hooked me up to the fetal heart monitor, and relief flooded over me when I heard the beautiful, comforting sound of her heartbeat.

Praise God!

But Dr. Evans' face looked grim. The staff was reserved, and I knew something wasn't right.

"If you don't have this baby as soon as possible, she won't be alive in three hours. You're having a fetal maternal hemorrhage. The placenta has failed."

"What? I'm not ready to have this baby!"

Dr. Evans was a warrior of a woman — an older, experienced OB/GYN physician who was voted one of

Child of Destiny

Seattle's best doctors in 2003 by her peers. She had been chief of staff at Overlake Hospital. I trusted her, completely. She looked at me with steady eyes that pled with me to be strong.

"*I'm* not ready for you to have this baby," she replied, grabbing my hand. "But if you don't have this baby right now, your baby is not going to make it."

Her tone told me that I didn't have a choice.

"Well, then, I guess I better call my husband and tell him we are having a baby today," I responded, desperately trying to process the information and to keep the panic out of my voice.

Dr. Evans smiled briefly, then whirled around to begin giving orders.

"Somebody go find me an anesthesiologist, stat! Get Maria in the operating room right now!" I had never seen her like that, and I knew the situation must be serious.

※ ※ ※

There wasn't time for the anesthesia to make me numb from the waist down. Though they put me out for the C-section, I woke up from the operation in extreme pain, feeling like my guts had been branded. It hurt too much to move, and I couldn't get off the surgery gurney for an entire day. They finally gave me some morphine so I'd be more comfortable.

Meanwhile, Jeff, who had received a panicked phone call and was able to rush to the hospital in time for our daughter's birth, accompanied Baby Elisha down to the NICU. Because of the hemorrhage, her blood had drained out, and she looked like a white ragdoll. She needed a blood transfusion in order to survive.

At the same time, Dr. Greg Romine, our dear friend and pastor, happened to be coming to Seattle for a couple of days to teach a class. When he heard about the dramatic delivery and complications, he came straight to the hospital. Jeff took him to see Elisha, all 5 pounds of her, hooked up to tubes and wires in an incubator. She had gone through the blood transfusion, but she wasn't out of danger.

"Can I put my hands on her and pray for her?" he asked the staff.

"Absolutely," they chimed.

Ever so gently, but with great intent, Dr. Greg placed his hands on our small baby girl and prayed that the healing power of Jesus would touch her tiny body. Her body changed as he prayed, and her skin pinked up even more with healthy color. God was performing a miracle as her life was being restored.

I was barely able to lift my head to see Elisha after she was born, so on the second day of her life, I felt well enough to sit in a wheelchair and roll down to the NICU to meet my daughter.

I will never forget the moment the nurses placed my Elisha Ramiah in my arms. She was surrounded in tubes, but she was the most beautiful thing I had ever seen. Her dark eyes met mine, and I could immediately see how

Child of Destiny

intelligent she was. She looked right into my eyes. It felt like she was looking straight into my soul.

"Hello, sweet baby," I cooed. "You are our precious 'child of destiny.' You were meant for our family. I will love you forever."

Very tenderly, I rocked my daughter, soaking in the moment I had waited a lifetime for. I breathed in the sweet aroma of her skin and listened to the squeaky noises she made with her soft voice. I held her little wrinkled fingers and marveled at her tiny fingernails.

I realized with great admiration just how many insurmountable odds this child had overcome in order to be born. God had definitely preserved this little girl until there was a safe place to plant her. Little had I known, when Dr. Ziga had prophesied our "child of destiny," or our friend Cyndi had written that "she is on the way," that there really was a two-cell soul on ice, just waiting patiently for her God-ordained moment in time.

~~~

Elisha only needed to stay in the NICU for a week before she got to come home with us and fill the little white cradle at the foot of our bed. While she had been premature, she grew at an amazing rate and was making all of her development benchmarks. We were so thankful for the doctors. Dr. Elisabeth Evans not only saved Elisha's life that day — she saved mine.

Life eventually settled into a routine, and motherhood

Souls on Ice

was all I hoped it would be. I continued running my ship supply business, and I wore Elisha in a carrier on my chest when I went down to the shipyard and even out onto the boats. She was a perfect companion at prayer meetings and potlucks. She fit easily into our lives, bringing us more joy than we had ever expected. She was a perfect baby with the sweetest countenance and a very easy-going personality.

Over the first couple years of her life, as I watched my "snowflake baby" achieve all of the normal infant and toddler milestones, I became painfully aware of how easily Elisha could have been discarded as an embryo, which would have robbed us of the chance to experience her beauty. Embryonic stem cell research, in particular, made my stomach churn. I didn't believe that embryos should be used for medical research. Adult stem cells were available as an alternative, so why on earth would scientists destroy and use embryos instead? What if Elisha's biological parents had chosen that option?

After a lot of thought, I decided to go to Washington, D.C., with my friend Kathie, to lobby agencies for a week or so. I wanted national pro-life organizations to hear my story so they could use it to make a case against the destruction of human embryos for research. My intention was to raise awareness about embryo adoption and argue against embryonic stem cell research.

While we were there, Kathie learned that Shirley Dobson of Focus on the Family just so happened to be staying at a hotel nearby. She would be attending the

Child of Destiny

National Day of Prayer activities with President Bush the following day.

Kathie got a wild idea.

"You should write a letter to President Bush, and see if Shirley Dobson will give it to him."

I knew we were going out on a limb, but I felt like it was worth a try. I penned a short note on Hilton Hotel stationary to President Bush, letting him know that I was in the city sowing seeds about embryo adoption. I thanked him for everything he was doing to bring awareness to the value of human life. I enclosed a picture of Elisha and attached the card to a small box of chocolates. I left it open for Mrs. Dobson to read and then wrote a nice note to her as well, asking her if she would kindly hand-deliver it to the president, if she had the opportunity and felt that it was appropriate. Then we left it all at the hotel's front desk, trusting that they would contact her and give her the special message.

A couple of weeks after we got back home, I received the following letter from the White House:

May 16, 2006

Dear Maria and Jeff:

Thank you for your nice letter and the pictures of your daughter, Elisha. I appreciate your kind words and prayers.

I applaud you for bringing Elisha into your life

Souls on Ice

and for giving her a loving family. Every human being is a precious gift of matchless value, and we must protect all our citizens at every stage of life.

Laura and I send our best wishes. Please accept the enclosed copy of the National Sanctity of Human Life Day proclamation. May God bless you, and may God continue to bless America.

Sincerely,
George W. Bush

I stood in my kitchen reading and re-reading the letter. I could hardly believe that Shirley Dobson had actually given him the package! It was almost too good to be true. I considered the trip a great success.

Jeff and I framed both the letter and the proclamation and hung them in our home. Feeling satisfied with my efforts, we went back to living our busy lives. We didn't know then that God was continuing to move. Our story was far from over.

ಞಞಞ

The rain came down in sheets, creating a muddy mess outside our barn. I readjusted the hood of my raincoat and headed back out into the downpour to get another horse. I needed to put horse blankets on all the horses — hard work made more difficult by the wet weather. I was becoming frustrated and irritable, not to mention muddy.

Child of Destiny

The phone was ringing in the barn, so I stopped my work to go answer it.

"Hello?" I was out of breath.

"Hello, is Maria Lancaster available?"

"This is she."

"Mrs. Lancaster, this is the White House."

My mouth dropped open.

Is this for real?

I was silent for a long moment while I let it sink in. I could hear the drumming of the raindrops on the tin barn roof.

"Good afternoon," I finally said.

"We received your name and phone number from Nightlight Christian Adoptions. The president is planning to veto Congress' bill approving the use of embryos in stem cell research. He would like to invite you and your family to the White House to appear onstage during his speech on Thursday and help put a face on embryo adoption."

I glanced down at my muddy clothes and boots. I couldn't believe this was happening. My mind was racing just thinking about the logistics. The White House was 3,000 miles away, and Elisha was so little. I wondered if it would be hard for us to make the trip.

But what an opportunity! Of course we would go! We would be honored.

The next 24 hours were a flurry of excitement. We booked our plane tickets and packed our bags. I didn't even have time to get my hair done or shop for a new

Souls on Ice

outfit. I figured my 20-year-old black suit would have to do. We got organized over the weekend, and flew out on Monday so we would have a few days to get our bearings before Thursday's big event.

It was a whirlwind of a week. We spent Tuesday and Wednesday meeting with legislators from around the country, including Senators Sam Brownback and Rick Santorum. It was so exciting to introduce our 2 1/2-year-old daughter to our lawmakers and explain her story. Other families who adopted embryos began to arrive, and all of us set out to talk to as many legislators as we could.

On Thursday morning, we were honored to be able to meet with President Bush privately before the big press conference. He looked very patriotic and presidential in his navy-blue suit and red tie. He greeted us with warmth, and I felt instinctively that before his office and position, his first identity was as a Christian, embracing us as fellow believers. He thanked us for having the guts to stand up publicly and expose ourselves. This was a big deal for him, too, having to rationalize saying no to funding embryonic stem cell research and disappoint his own party after they passed a bill to fund it. It was the first veto of his five years in office.

After the White House photographer took our picture with the president, I handed Elisha a birthday card that she was to give to him. He had just celebrated his 60th birthday. Jeff was holding her at the time, and she very dramatically presented the card to President Bush, then put her arm around his neck and pulled him close to her.

Then, without warning, she kissed him squarely on the lips.

I was shocked, but the president just chuckled.

"Well, that's the best thing that has happened to me all day!"

❧❧❧

My eyes traveled over the famous and historic East Room, noting the astonishing amount of gold-colored furnishings. From the sconces on the walls to the heavy curtains behind the stage where we sat, everything in the room spoke of its intimidating grandeur. Abraham Lincoln was laid out in this very room in his casket. I studied the massive, brightly lit chandeliers hanging from the high ceiling and decided with certainty that I had never before been in a room as majestic as this one. There were leaders from every state in the nation, and countless media outlets were there to hear what the president had to say.

I turned my attention back to the president's speech.

"We must also remember that embryonic stem cells come from human embryos that are destroyed for their cells. Each of these human embryos is a unique human life with inherent dignity and matchless value. We see that value in the children who are with us today. Each of these children began his or her life as a frozen embryo that was created for in vitro fertilization but remained unused after the fertility treatments were complete. Each of these children was adopted while still an embryo and has been blessed with a chance to grow — to grow up in a loving family. These boys and girls are not spare parts. They remind us of what is lost when embryos are destroyed in the name of research. They remind us that we all begin our lives as a small collection of cells. And they remind us that in our zeal of new treatments and cures, America must never abandon our fundamental morals."

"These boys and girls are not spare parts." Oh, how I love that!

When the speech ended, they chose two families to go out and address the media. They picked Jeff, Elisha and me as one of those families.

We stood on the White House lawn under a large oak tree and answered a variety of questions about the adoption and our family life.

"We have to call our family and tell them what's going on — *before* the 6 o'clock news," I whispered to Jeff when it was over. Our family and friends still didn't know we had adopted Elisha as an embryo. As far as they knew, she was biologically ours.

"It's too late." He grinned. "It was a *live* broadcast!"

"Well, when we get home, we are going to have to call a family meeting and explain why this all unfolded the way that it did."

Our big, cherished family secret had just become the world's business.

Child of Destiny

∻∻∻

Surprisingly enough, our family didn't mind at all. They loved Elisha, and it didn't matter to them that she had been adopted as a frozen embryo. We did have some friends who saw the broadcast and were quite shocked. But regardless, it felt better having it out in the open, especially since I was beginning to feel that I should become an even more vocal advocate for embryo adoption. Our privacy was worth sacrificing so people could understand that embryos are human life. They needed to know that they could be adopted and live!

A few months later, Ron Stoddart, the executive director for Nightlight Christian Adoptions, approached me and said that President Bush had authorized a $1,000,000 grant for embryo adoption awareness. He asked if I would work for them, traveling around the Northwest for a year, visiting fertility clinics and helping to spread awareness. I agreed.

The same year, I was also named the Washington State Coordinator for the National Prayer Task Force and needed to travel to Focus on the Family's headquarters in Colorado Springs to participate in a task force meeting. I brought Elisha along and found the opportunity to introduce her to Dr. James Dobson himself, the very one whose radio program had been the catalyst for our adoption journey. He was pleased to meet Elisha, and I thanked him for performing the radio interview that changed our lives. If it weren't for Dr. Dobson, Elisha may still be frozen in a lab in North Carolina, one of hundreds of thousands of nameless individuals waiting for their destinies to start.

❧❧❧

Part of my job with the awareness grant included organizing a regional event on a tight budget. I needed a venue, and as I racked my brain over places that would be feasible for the event, I remembered Cedar Park Church, the church where Jeff and I had gone for prayer on that Presentation Sunday so many years before. It had a lovely chapel and facility that would be perfect. I called up the pastor, Dr. Joe Fuiten.

"I was wondering if we could use your chapel facility for an event we're holding regarding embryo adoption." I held my breath. I fully expected him to brush me off or reject me entirely.

"Sure!" the pastor responded.

I was shocked but thrilled. "Do you think you'd also be available to open the meeting and give your own story about infertility?" I knew that he and his wife had suffered through multiple miscarriages before eventually having four children. That was why Presentation Sunday was such a big deal to him.

Much to my delight, Dr. Fuiten agreed to open the meeting. It was a cause close to his heart, and I believed he was the perfect person to do it.

The event went well, and afterward, I stood at my

booth, handing out VHS tapes with information about embryo adoption. Dr. Fuiten came up and looked at my materials, and we made light small talk.

"You know what?" I said to him during a brief lull at my table. "You should start an embryo adoption agency, and I'll run it for you."

The words flew out of my mouth before I even realized what I was saying, but Dr. Fuiten didn't even flinch. He just looked at me, his gaze even.

"Well, why don't you make an appointment with my assistant, and let's talk about it."

So I did. Over the next year, Dr. Fuiten and I had a series of meetings — first laying out the philosophy and mission statement of the agency, then digging into the nuts and bolts on the business end.

Taking our cue from Nightlight and the few other agencies that existed, we knew our pricing had to be significantly lower than the IVF process, or infertile couples wouldn't even consider it. Not only did we want to reduce the number of frozen embryos out there, but we also wanted to do our part in encouraging people to choose embryo adoption over IVF. *Why make more embryos,* I thought, *while there are so many already in the freezer?*

There was a lot that had to be decided, from liability insurance and payroll down to the very process our clients would go through to adopt. We needed to have a social worker on staff, as well as a counselor.

We decided to call our agency Embryo Adoption

Souls on Ice

Services of Cedar Park, and it was going to be the first church-based embryo adoption service in the world. We set November 9, 2008 as our target start date, but there was still plenty of work to do.

≈≈≈

In the meantime, the 2008 presidential election process was in full swing, and former Arkansas Governor Mike Huckabee was running for the Republican ticket. He came through Seattle on his campaign trail. Pastor Fuiten was actively involved in helping to promote his campaign, and I knew his pro-life stance, so I decided to attend his press conference. As I drove down the gravel drive of our place, I felt like God wanted me to go back in the house and get a wallet-sized photo of Elisha to give to Governor Huckabee. I felt like I should tell him the story, if possible.

After the customary speeches and remarks, there was a receiving line, and I did meet Governor Huckabee. I thanked him for being a leader in the pro-life movement. I hesitated, and he kept on going down the line of people. Dread came over me — the kind of dread when you realize on your way to the airport that your plane ticket to Hawaii was for yesterday. With that, and a new dose of courage, I set out to track him down in the meeting hall. I caught up with him, weaving my way through the cameras and media.

"Mr. Huckabee, I'm sorry, but I must tell you this story." I pulled out a picture of Elisha dressed in an old-

Child of Destiny

fashioned lace dress and pearl necklace, holding tightly to a teddy bear. "I want you to meet this child," I continued. "My husband and I adopted her as a frozen embryo, and she was in a freezer for four years at two cells. Her name is Elisha, and she's my daughter."

Governor Huckabee took the picture and looked at Elisha's beautiful face.

"That is amazing," he answered. He looked squarely at me, his eyes wide, and said, "This changes everything."

"You can keep the picture, Mr. Huckabee. And I hope that when people argue with you over whether an embryo is a human life, you will show them Elisha's picture and explain to them that every embryo is a human life." I could feel the urgency and passion in my voice, but it didn't seem to faze him.

"I will carry it," he promised, tucking Elisha's picture into his wallet. "Thank you very much."

"Thank *you*," I said, shaking his hand with genuine gratitude.

ಌಌಌ

Our launch date for the adoption agency was quickly approaching, and a week before we were scheduled to open, my friends Peggy and Walt sent me a news article from the *Los Angeles Times* about embryo adoption. I forwarded it to Pastor Fuiten. We decided that in light of the subject hitting the news in such a timely way, we should send out a press release making people aware that we had an embryo adoption agency in Seattle. We could piggy-back on their media coverage. And maybe we would get a media miracle.

The Seattle Times came out to our ranch and took pictures and videos for three days. They photographed 5-year-old Elisha in a dress of pink tulle and followed her around as she rode bareback on her sorrel horse, Oso. She was her normal self — showing her captivating and charming personality.

How could anyone not fall in love with Elisha? I thought.

It was a fairly liberal newspaper, so I was interested as to what kind of spin they would put on our story.

Six days after the launch of Embryo Adoption Services of Cedar Park, Elisha and I went down to the shipyard on a Friday morning where I had to get some work done. Next to the docks was a breakfast place called the Bay Café, and we hurried over, hoping to get a glance at the newspapers in the stands out front. I was still walking up when I saw the bold headline.

"New Life" was the headline of *The Seattle Times*.

Are you kidding me?

Elisha squealed with delight as I searched through my coin purse for some quarters. We were both so excited, it was hard not to drop change all over the dock. When at last I had found enough, I stuck them in the slot and opened the stand, grabbing the prized newspaper with my little girl's picture on the front.

The article was well done. Of course, they also had to

Child of Destiny

show the pro-choice angle, but the story was great. I was overjoyed. Within a few days, it had gone viral.

At Embryo Adoption Services of Cedar Park, the phone rang off the hook. Calls came in from all over the world! We had a pile of clients right away, and it was very exciting. We had donor families wanting to make their extra embryos available, and we had infertile families wanting to know more about the process.

From the very beginning, it was obvious to me that God's hand was guiding every single adoption and every single match. Donor families and adoptive families would each send in their picture profiles, and it was my job to match them to one another. There was an amazing responsibility that came with making sure the right embryos were matched with the right family — that where they ended up would make sense to the kids someday. I prayed over each situation and solicited the prayers of others as well. Our social worker also met with the families, conducting home studies just as they would with a traditional adoption.

❧❧❧

We had so many interesting things happen, we knew God was part of the matching process. He knew which embryos were to be in each home — it was just our job to pray and try to figure that part out.

I was amazed that an embryo would be donated with half-Chinese, half-Caucasian genetics, and within days, I had received a profile from an adopting couple that was half-Chinese and half-Caucasian. Only God could line that up.

We had many matches that were specific racial matches: Hispanic, Japanese, Chinese, African-American, Caucasian, etc. It was so interesting how God would bring these families together at just the right time in our program. We realized prayer, above all things, was the key to the matching process. The matching process was the true grace of God.

We believe that God has a specific plan for each child's life and that he has a specific time and place he wants him or her to be born. I thought about John the Baptist and how God had spoken through prophets hundreds of years in advance, telling the world that he would come to announce the coming Messiah, Jesus. He had a specific job for John to do — to prepare the way for our Savior Jesus Christ. In order for that to take place, John had to be born first, and he had to be Jesus' cousin.

In the same way, it's clear that God has ordained certain children to be born to certain families at certain times for reasons only known to him. I just felt honored to be a part of the process.

ماماما

The day our agency's first baby was delivered was a thrilling one. It was March of 2010. It suddenly felt so real — that the decisions we made in matching families and coordinating the transfer of embryos were resulting in *real babies*. Real *people*.

Julian was a handsome little prince and his parents, Brian and Melanie, were thrilled. They came all the way from Chicago to let us all see their "child of destiny." It was the most rewarding thing I had ever been a part of in my entire life. The matches just kept coming, and I was constantly astonished at how God worked out every single one of them.

A Hispanic couple in Washington had done IVF and given birth to twins with one embryo left un-transferred. The father was in a wheelchair, and it was just not possible for them to take care of any more children. I was able to match the embryo with a wonderful couple in Texas: a Caucasian pastor and his Hispanic wife. They had a beautiful baby boy that looked just like his mom.

An extraordinarily tall husband and wife in Texas donated their embryos, and I matched them with a 5-foot, 11-inch pediatrician and her 6-foot, 2-inch husband in Oklahoma. Their adopted child, likely to be tall because of her genes, need never feel too tall or out of place in her own home.

We found Japanese families for Japanese embryos and all other kinds of similar ethnic matches. We felt it was in the best interest of the children to be in a family that shared characteristics with the donating family.

Then there was another little boy born in Illinois after 13 years in the freezer! The donor father lost his wife and was raising twin 13-year-old girls. His pastor advised him

Souls on Ice

to donate the remaining embryos to another family, and now a miracle boy was born. The sorrow of his wife's passing was eased by the birth of the miracle boy. And what about another family in Illinois, whose twin girls were born after a decade in the freezer? Who but God can do it? So many amazing stories!

Every single match story was a miracle in the making.

It reminded me of the scripture I loved in Psalm 64:9: "Everyone shall stand in awe and confess the greatness of the miracle of God … They will realize what amazing things he does."

❧❧❧

Mike Huckabee contacted us about a year after we first met and asked if our family would share our story as part of a movie he was making with Citizens United, an organization that creates documentaries. They sent a film crew and director Kevin Knoblock from LA to our home for the interview. We were able to share the whole story of how Elisha came to be. I was excited to learn that many other people I admired and respected for their work in defending the unborn were also going to be included in the movie.

When *The Gift of Life* documentary was finished, they sent us an advance copy. We watched it as a family, and tears streamed down my cheeks as I remembered the day I gave Mike Huckabee Elisha's photograph. *I am so glad I gave him that picture,* I thought.

Child of Destiny

In December of 2011, *The Gift of Life* premiered at Hoyt Sherman Place in Des Moines, Iowa. A beautifully adorned, newly restored theater, it seated about 800 people. Jeff, Elisha and I flew out for the big debut, as well as Pastor Fuiten and other friends. Because the presidential debates were going on during that time, we met all the candidates running for president. The real fun, however, was when Mike Huckabee showed Elisha that he still carried her picture in his wallet. She beamed like a princess when he pulled out her photo.

"I still have your picture, Elisha, and I will always carry it," he said warmly.

I was amazed that sharing her picture had led to this momentous day. God had a hand in allowing me the opportunities to share my story and to educate political leaders about the miracle of embryo adoption and the sanctity of human life.

Jeff and I were seeing history unfold before our eyes, and it was amazing. I sat next to Newt Gingrich, Governor Rick Perry, Michelle Bachman, Rick Santorum and a long list of conservative heavyweights. It was awesome to share the joy of the debut of this great pro-life documentary with such inspiring people and the other people and inspiring stories featured in it.

༄༄༄

By the time we celebrated the fifth anniversary of Embryo Adoption Services of Cedar Park in November of

Souls on Ice

2013, we had seen dozens of children come into the world through our ministry. In addition, there were nine more adoptive mothers who were pregnant and a dozen more waiting for their adoptions to be finalized before transfers could take place. People usually found out about our program and ministry through Internet searches, doctor referrals or family and friends telling them about it. It was important to us to make our fees very reasonable to encourage embryo adoption, and we were happy that so many fertility clinics were glad to work with us. We definitely had a lot to celebrate. We had opportunities to pray with people struggling with infertility and to bring the hope and love of Jesus to their hearts and homes.

One of the most beautiful parts about embryo donation for adoption is helping the adopting and donating families meet each other. Not all families have open adoptions, but for some families, it is a great fit. If it is in the best interest of the child, we work to introduce families when the time is right. Being able to have an open adoption is a gift from God, and it is a gift to be able to love another family for the sake of the embryos and born children.

❧❧❧

On a lovely summer evening in 2013, Elisha and I gathered in a Seattle park with adoptive parents, Kate and Jason, so their baby, Liam, could meet his biological family. We sat on a blanket under a grove of tall trees, while Lisa and Mark took turns holding the baby that looked so much like them and their young son, Joshua.

What a strangely cool thing it is that Liam and Joshua will grow up knowing each other — biological brothers, but in two different, terrific families!

We spread out a picnic dinner, and I watched Kate dote on little Liam, thanking Lisa again and again for the precious gift she had given her. Liam was loved very much. I sat back on the blanket, just relishing every moment of the reunion.

"Oh, he's so handsome!" Lisa cooed, caressing his brown infant-sized jogging suit. "I just can't get over it! Hello, little Liam."

Liam flashed her his adorable toothless grin, and everyone laughed. Kate just beamed. Her eyes sparkled with the bliss of motherhood — a feeling I knew very well.

I watched my own Elisha skip across the park, her chestnut-brown hair flying behind her. She had such a happy spirit and had brought so much joy to Jeff and me over the past decade. I couldn't imagine our lives without her. She was my longing fulfilled — my tree of life.

If I had never had Elisha, these other children wouldn't have been born, either, I thought wistfully.

What an incredible thought that was! God had had bigger plans than even *we* realized when he promised us our "child of destiny." It wasn't all about our infertility and my desire to be a mother. It wasn't all about Elisha, though we were certain God's plans for her life were uniquely wonderful.

It was also about Liam and the many hundreds of

Souls on Ice

other embryo adoptions Elisha's birth would eventually inspire. It was about filling the arms of hopeful parents with their own children of destiny.

And, most importantly, it was about all the hundreds of thousands of souls on ice for which, one by one, God was orchestrating *life*.

> "At the time of sacrifice, the prophet Elijah stepped forward and prayed: 'Lord, the God of Abraham, Isaac and Israel, let it be known today that you are God in Israel and that I am your servant and have done all these things at your command. Answer me, Lord, answer me, so these people will know that you, Lord, are God, and that you are turning their hearts back again.'" (I Kings 18:36-37)

A pregnant Maria Lancaster awaiting her child of destiny

The Lancasters

80

Child of Destiny

Maria's first time celebrating Mother's Day as a mom

Elisha Lancaster

Elisha and her pony

Souls on Ice

Elisha, Maria and Jeff Lancaster

Maria, Elisha and Jeff Lancaster with former
President George Bush at the White House

Child of Destiny

Jeff and Maria at *The Gift of Life* movie premiere, De Moines, Iowa, December 2011

Maria and Elisha with Newt Gingrich at *The Gift of Life* premiere, December 2011

Jeff, Maria and Elisha with Rick Santorum at *The Gift of Life* premiere

Souls on Ice

Mike Huckabee shows Elisha the picture he still carries of her in his wallet

Elisha Lancaster with Dr. James Dobson in 2009

Elisha on her horse, on the front page of the *Seattle Times*, November 20, 2008 - headline NEW LIFE!

Waiting
The Adoption Story of Rachel and Diony Victorin
Written by Angela Welch Prusia

I saw my daughter before her birth.

In my vision, she twirled before me with all the innocence of a 3 year old. Caramel-colored ringlets of hair and light brown skin made her the perfect mix of her father's Haitian roots and my Caucasian background.

Esther. Her name would be Esther. Like the Jewish queen in the Bible.

The name had resonated deep within my spirit since reading the book in the Old Testament one night when I couldn't sleep.

"What do you think of naming our daughter Esther?" I asked my husband, Diony. Like me, he had a dream where he saw my stomach, swollen with child. Lying in his arms while we imagined our future children, I couldn't be happier.

"It's perfect," he agreed.

Esther had yet to be born. But the prospect of motherhood — one of my deepest desires — thrilled me.

Everything I did revolved around children — teaching Sunday school, volunteering at summer camps, working with social services and now my employment as a pediatric nurse.

Souls on Ice

After years of marriage, I could think of little else. I resisted the urge to fill our future nursery with tiny shoes and adorable outfits. Every baby I saw in the clinic kicked in my mothering urges.

Each month, I eagerly awaited the results of yet another home pregnancy test. I searched for the pink lines till my eyes crossed from staring at the tests so long. Disappointment hit with each failed attempt.

After nearly half a year without results, I mentioned my concern to my doctor.

"You know, you would be an older mom," she reminded me. "Maybe we should do some testing."

Her suggestion seemed reasonable enough, but we wanted to proceed cautiously. As Christians, Diony and I spent time together asking God what was best for our family.

෴෴෴

We decided to visit a fertility specialist for a consultation in June of 2008. The possibility of being pregnant with our child appealed to me. After talking with the doctor, Diony remembered long-forgotten details from his dream years earlier. He hurried to check his journal before sharing more with me.

"Look, Rachel." Diony pointed to his prayer journal. "It's right here."

Since I can't read French, he translated.

"I didn't understand the dream at the time," he rushed

Waiting

in his excitement. "But when I saw you pregnant, I saw the Petri dish from the process the fertility doctor just described."

My heart swelled with hope.

Visualize the child I will bring you. God's voice sounded in my spirit.

I cut baby pictures from magazines and glued them onto a piece of construction paper I posted on the bathroom mirror. It felt a little weird, but seeing the children gave me hope.

"It's natural to feel nervous," our doctor encouraged us during the next visit. His wise face brought me comfort.

I wiped my palms on the hospital gown. Fear competed with my hope. *What if the procedure doesn't work?* I'd read enough literature to know the birth rates from a single cycle of in vitro gave me a 30 to 40 percent success rate. The percentages declined after age 35 — my age.

"We start with hormone treatments to shut down your pituitary gland," the doctor said, explaining the procedure to us. "Then you will receive hormone injections."

He looked at me with eyes full of compassion. He knew the process would be emotionally and physically demanding. "Are you ready?" he asked.

I gulped down my fear and nodded. Diony squeezed my hand.

The next three weeks demanded more than I'd imagined. The physical pain brought me to tears, while the emotional toll rendered me a wreck. I refused to give up.

Souls on Ice

"We're going to sedate you," my doctor explained before taking me to surgery. "An ultrasound will help guide me. After a few days, we'll transfer the embryo into you."

I prayed that the process would work. I wanted so badly to be a mom. *Mom.* The word tasted so sweet. Thoughts of our baby filled me as I drifted off into sedated sleep.

☙☙☙

Two weeks later, anticipation threatened my sanity. Every twinge or bout with nausea made me wonder if I was pregnant. When I saw the doctor's office number on my caller ID, I gripped the phone in my hand, afraid to breathe.

"Hi, Rachel," the in vitro coordinator greeted me.

My hope sank. I could read the sadness in her voice. "I'm so sorry. You're not pregnant."

My lip trembled.

"Don't give up hope," she reassured me. "It's common not to get pregnant on the first round."

Diony wrapped his arms around me. "I'm so sorry, love. Remember what God said over and over in the Old Testament. Be strong and courageous. Don't be afraid."

I clung to God's words, spoken through my husband.

"God will give us a child, Rachel." Diony didn't let go of me. "We have to believe his promise to us."

Waiting

I remembered my vision of Esther. Our little girl was coming. I had to believe.

"Every promise comes with trials. That's why God reminds us to be strong and not afraid."

I wiped the tears from my eyes and breathed a prayer. *Help me, Jesus. I don't want to be afraid.*

❧❧❧

The next three rounds brought more bad news. I wasn't pregnant.

A false positive on Valentine's Day crushed me. I'd brought roses to the office at the school where Diony worked. "Happy Valentine's Day, babe. You're going to be a father."

He'd grabbed me in an embrace. Our hopes had soared.

I'd repeated the gesture with my mom, Nell, telling her she would be a grandmother. She and my dad, Pete, had been so excited for me to have a baby. Diony's family in Haiti and Florida were also praying constantly for us, believing God would bring us a child.

But two days later, my hormone levels dropped. The embryo had implanted but stopped growing. My body reacted as if I'd miscarried, and the resulting postpartum depression sent me reeling.

Tears sprang to my eyes at the slightest thought of babies — as a pediatric nurse, the reminder was constant. At home, I stared at the diapers, outfits and the blanket

Souls on Ice

with the star pattern I had purchased to swaddle our miracle.

Lord, I don't know if I can take anymore.

Maybe adoption was the answer. After all, my parents had adopted my brother, Jason, as an infant. Love formed a bond as strong as any biological tie.

I thought about my foster brother, Lamell. He'd come to live with us at age 10. Years later, I couldn't imagine our lives without him in our family.

I turned on the radio alarm clock before lying down to sleep.

… thousands of embryos await adoption …

A broadcast from Focus on the Family caught my attention. I turned up the volume and sat on the bed. Diony leaned closer, a big smile on his face.

"They're called snowflake babies," he said. "I heard the same show earlier in the day."

I listened intently, captivated by the idea. I'd never thought much about the unused embryos remaining after the process of in vitro fertilization.

The show ended, and Diony reached for my hands. "This may be the answer, Rachel. After I heard the broadcast, I told God if this was his plan then he would have to tell you."

Hope burst into my heart. I couldn't wait to do more research.

Waiting

"I'm sorry, Rachel."

Our frozen embryo didn't develop inside my womb.

The familiar words struck me with finality. My knees buckled under me, and I collapsed into my supervisor's arms. I'd confided my struggles to get pregnant with her and another coworker. They sent me home for the rest of the afternoon.

Shards of my broken dreams pierced my heart. Diony and I couldn't have a baby who shared our combined genetic makeup. I believed in the furthest recesses of my spirit that God had a baby for us. But the devastating news made holding onto hope tough.

Diony prayed to God faithfully three times a day, like Daniel in the Bible. He encouraged me on the hardest days.

The year before, we'd attended an infertility prayer service at Cedar Park Church. Several churches in the area held special vigils each year for couples like us who struggled with getting pregnant. The prayers and stories had renewed hope in both me and Diony.

When I had seen Maria Lancaster, the director for Embryo Adoption Services of Cedar Park, at the service the year before, I remembered an article featured in *The Seattle Times.* Her daughter, Elisha, who she and her husband had adopted as an embryo, had just started kindergarten. I decided to ask Maria more about embryo adoption.

"Do you have any biracial embryos?" I asked.

"Unfortunately, no." She shook her head sadly. "I wish I could answer differently."

After our embryo transfer had failed, I checked an agency in California. Soon after, something compelled me to ask Maria in Seattle.

"Hi, Maria. It's Rachel again." I left a message on her machine. "Just wanted to check if any biracial embryos had been donated yet."

Not long after, I could hear Maria's excitement through the phone.

"Rachel, I think this might be an answer from God."

I inhaled, trying to stifle my hopes. I couldn't bear more bad news.

"We just accepted a set of embryos from a multiracial couple three days ago."

I nearly dropped the phone.

❦❦❦

"Look at you in that picture." I pointed to a silly shot of my husband and laughed. The sound was a welcome change after our two-year rollercoaster ride with disappointment.

He selected a picture of us on the beach. "Let's include this one."

I smiled. The beach was our favorite place to visit. It seemed only fitting to include the picture in the book we put together to introduce ourselves to the genetic parents of our new baby.

Waiting

When we finished, I sat at the computer to compose an introduction letter.

Nervous energy kept my stomach in knots for days. We'd finished the home study and background checks like any adoption; now we just waited to see if the donors would select us from the other potential adoptive families.

When Maria called, I could barely breathe. The suspense nearly undid me.

"Congratulations! Jodi and Larry have selected you and Diony to adopt their embryos." I could hear her smile through the phone. "They love the beach, too."

I could barely speak. *How could words express my deep-felt gratitude?*

I read the letter from the donors, treasuring every word.

Hello,

I'll start by saying how happy we are to have found a couple we can help. We are very excited for our little embryos to have a chance at life!!

I'll tell you a little about us.

My husband and I have known each other for almost 19 years now. Larry (Lawrence) asked me to marry him Christmas Eve. I said yes. We flew to Louisiana where my father lived, and we got married by a lake in my dad's hometown. My father (Bobby) soon after found out he had lung cancer, and he passed. Larry and I had been pregnant two times during the first year and a half of our relationship, but both pregnancies ended (blighted ovums) so we kind of gave up. We spent our time traveling to see family all over and working ... until I read about IVF over the Web.

Larry did not have any children, and I had a son from a previous relationship, and we wanted to have a child together so we gave IVF a shot and got pregnant on the first try. It was a blessing from God!! We had every intention of one day trying again ourselves, but I had some uterine problems and had to have a hysterectomy this year.

We have struggled with what to do about the embryos for a long time. We didn't want them to be discarded or used for study, and we didn't feel comfortable with a family having them that we couldn't know about, so when I came across the Embryo Adoption page over the Web, I was very happy and hoping for this to be the answer! With that ... I am happy to say I think our prayer has been answered!

We would like to have some form of contact. Of course, we would like to know if there is a viable pregnancy and ultimately a baby. Pictures and a letter or two would be nice, and maybe one day your children and ours can meet.

We are very happy and excited!!

I'll end here for now and let God do the rest.

Larry & Jodi

Waiting

❧❧❧

Diony and I were especially surprised to learn that Jodi and Larry had gone to the same fertility clinic. Our embryos had slept near one another.

In February of 2011, Diony held my hand as the embryo transfer took place. We left the office to endure the agony of waiting. *Would we really have a baby this time?*

When the news came that I was pregnant, my excitement competed with fear. *Was this another false positive?* Still it was hard not to imagine sweet baby kisses and precious lullabies.

A few weeks passed before severe pain rocked my body, waking me in the middle of the night. Blood seeped through my clothing. I curled up on our bed, sure that we'd lost the baby. Devastation shook my faith once again.

The next morning, I dragged myself to the fertility clinic. Tears stained my cheeks and left blood-red lines in the whites of my eyes. I braced myself for the worst.

Instead the sweetest sound filled my ears.

Thump. Thump. Thump. The tiny heartbeat echoed throughout the room. Relief swept over me. "Thank you, God!" I sobbed.

"Your baby is okay, but part of the lining has separated from your uterus," the doctor cautioned. "It's possible that you could miscarry. I recommend that you rest, so your body can heal."

I called work immediately. Nothing would stand in the

Souls on Ice

way of me protecting this baby. Back home, Diony propped pillows on our couch and kissed my head. His affection touched me. I could already imagine him showing the same tenderness to our baby. "You're going to make a great father."

"Get some rest." He kissed me and turned down the lights. "Hang in there, love. God is going to help us through this."

❧ ❧ ❧

"You have to pray with me," I told a few close friends who I knew would fight alongside us. "Believe with me that I won't miscarry.

"In all things, God, you work for the good of us who love you and have been called according to your purpose." I recited favorite verses in Romans and Jeremiah. "You have plans to give me hope and a future."

When I was 12 weeks pregnant, the ultrasound showed a healthy baby, and my care was transferred to an OB/GYN doctor. My heart soared.

I continued to exercise caution. Morning sickness was intense, but it was nothing compared to everything I'd experienced. Nothing could take away my joy. All the earlier heartache was worth becoming a mommy.

Emotions still continued to send us on a rollercoaster ride. A test revealed I had a 25 percent chance of having a child with Down syndrome. Because of our faith, abortion wasn't an option. I refused to do an amniocentesis test. I

Waiting

didn't want to risk miscarrying the baby we learned was a little girl.

I wrestled with having a child with special needs. "Lord, please bless us with a healthy baby," I prayed. "But even if this child has Down's, we know you gave us this baby. We will praise you and help raise this baby to bring you glory."

In July, swelling made work difficult, and my blood pressure spiked. In early September, when I bent over and saw stars, my doctor admitted me to the hospital with preeclampsia. Two weeks later, my blood pressure skyrocketed.

"Even though it's a little bit early," my doctor explained, "your blood pressure is too great a risk. We need to induce labor."

After 51 hours of labor and three hours of pushing, exhaustion threatened to break me.

"Your little one is stuck," the doctor explained. "We need to do a C-section."

Diony squeezed my hand. He knew my desire for a natural delivery, but we deferred to the doctor's expertise.

The nurses hurried to prep me for surgery. The pain medication made me nauseous and miserable. The prep and C-section lasted all of 30 minutes. I couldn't wait for the nausea to end and to meet our sweet baby.

"Here she is," the doctor's words met my ears.

I craned my neck to see, but the curtain blocked my view. "Is she okay?" Worry crept into my voice. I didn't hear a cry. "Does she have Down syndrome?"

Souls on Ice

"You have a healthy baby girl." A nurse held the sweetest miracle up for me to see.

"Hey there, Esther Hope." Tears leaked down my face. Dark hair framed her perfect features.

Every ounce of my being wanted to cradle my baby next to my heart, but I was just too ill to hold her. My blood pressure spiked to dangerous levels and seizures became a possibility.

Thankfully, Esther could stay in my room while I stayed at the hospital for the next seven days. I couldn't stop staring at my sweet little girl. Gratitude overwhelmed me. I could hardly contain the love which welled up inside me. I was finally a mother.

॰॰॰

When Esther turned 3 months old, I couldn't shake the desire for her to get to know her other family. My adopted brother didn't meet his biological parents until age 30, and I'd seen the hole he'd had in his life. I knew that longing also filled my brother, Lamell, as he missed his biological family.

I contacted Maria, and she received permission from the donors to share their contact information with us. Jodi and I exchanged e-mails and texts before she called me one afternoon as I rocked Esther.

Talking to Jodi cemented the deal. When she shared similarities between her daughter, Bobbie, and Esther, I couldn't wait to meet her.

Waiting

"Let's do this. Let's meet somewhere."

We decided to meet at McDonald's in Federal Way, halfway between both our homes.

❧❧❧

When I stepped toward the dark-haired woman watching her daughter play, a peace flooded my spirit. Jodi introduced me to 3-year-old Bobbie. Esther showed an uncanny resemblance to her.

Larry and I exchanged introductions.

"Do you want to hold Esther?" I handed her to Jodi. Her tenderness touched me.

"She's beautiful." Tears welled in Jodi's eyes.

No one spoke, each lost in the miracle taking place.

When Larry took Esther, I could tell he was a great dad.

I knelt down to Bobbie's level. She was so excited to see the baby.

"This is Esther," Jodi explained to Bobbie. "She's a special part of our family." Bobbie was fascinated by her tiny fingers and toes. She sweetly held Esther's hand as we spent the next hour and a half learning more about each other.

Before we left, Jodi and I promised to get the girls together. Diony had missed our first meeting due to work, but we made plans to see each other again. When we embraced, I knew that the day marked the first of many special moments together.

Souls on Ice

❦❦❦

I dialed the now-familiar number.

"Esther won't take a pacifier," I told Jodi over the phone. "I give her one when she's fussy, but she just spits it out."

Jodi laughed. "That's exactly like Bobbie."

I loved talking to Jodi. There was so much to learn about being a mom. Her invaluable experience meant the world to me, especially given her added insight into my little girl.

Watching the girls interact together on monthly play dates mesmerized us both, and we started calling them sisters.

A year after our relationship developed, we had a question for Jodi and Larry. "What do you think of Esther calling you Mama Jodi and Papa Larry?"

Pleasure replaced their surprise. "We'd like that."

❦❦❦

"Happy 1st birthday, Esther," Jodi's mom, Grandma Norma, and Larry's mom, Grandma Pookey, sang out. Grandpa Larry, Larry's dad, was disappointed he couldn't make the party. He adores Esther.

"You are one loved little girl." Jodi's mom kissed Esther on her forehead. She's unofficially adopted me and Diony, and the entire family has welcomed the three of us into their hearts.

Waiting

Each milestone is so much fun celebrating together with our new extended family. Pictures and videos bear witness to our many moments together.

Last Christmas, Jodi invited Esther to participate in their cookie-frosting tradition.

Esther sat on Larry's lap — right next to her big sister. When Bobbie licked the frosting, Esther followed. She stuck her finger into the container and tasted the frosting, her eyes big with pleasure. We couldn't stop laughing at her messy face.

Seeing Esther's special bond with Bobbie only fuels our desire to continue living life together.

⁕⁕⁕

"*People* magazine called the office today," Maria Lancaster told me over the phone. "They want to do a story. I think Esther's story would be perfect to share."

Mixed emotions made me exhale. Esther's story was beautiful. *But were we willing to sacrifice our privacy? What about Esther's safety?*

"Can I get back with you?" I asked. "Diony and I need to pray."

We spent the next several days seeking God's direction. In the end, we felt Esther's story needed to be told. She was the face of thousands of embryos waiting to be adopted into loving homes. Like her namesake, God rescued her, and he would use her for "such a time as this."

Souls on Ice

❦❦❦

On December 17, 2012, Esther's story came out in *People* magazine. Given Esther's royal heritage in the Bible, it seemed fitting the cover would feature Prince William and Kate's announcement of their coming baby.

Esther is one of the most amazing gifts we've ever been given. Diony and I still stand in awe of the opportunity we were given to be her parents.

We know that life is precious. Esther is living proof. She is nearly the age she was when I first saw her in my dream twirling around, ringlet curls bouncing and caramel skin glowing.

Not long after my vision of Esther, I saw myself holding a 3-month-old baby boy.

Our son.

Daniel.

His name will be Daniel. My husband's Bible hero, a man of prayer.

I long to kiss my son's precious cheeks.

His daddy and I dream of the day we get to bring him home.

> "Satisfy us in the morning with your unfailing love, so we may sing for joy to the end of our lives. Give us gladness in proportion to our former misery! Replace the evil years with good. Let us see your miracles again; let our children see your glory at work. And may the Lord our God show us his approval and make our efforts successful. Yes, make our efforts successful!" (Psalm 90:14-17 NLT)

Waiting

The Victorins and Esther Hope

The Answer

The Donating Story of Jodi and Larry Dillworth
Written by Angela Welch Prusia

A baby's cry broke the fog of my anesthesia. I blinked, taking in the sterile hospital room. The hint of baby lotion made me smile.

"It's okay, sweet girl." My husband, Larry, rocked our newborn in his arms not far from my bed. His attempt to feed her met with more tears.

"Want some help?" I propped myself to a sitting position.

"She's been so fussy." Larry handed the dark-haired bundle to me, his nerves as a new father evident. We'd named her Bobbie after my father who'd lost his battle to cancer a year before her arrival.

"Hey, pretty girl." I kissed Bobbie's nose. "You don't want to eat?"

She stopped crying as I talked to her. I remembered little after the C-section, so I treasured these first moments with my daughter.

"Let me look at you."

I lay Bobbie gently on the bed while Larry took a seat beside us. Pride shone from his eyes. "She's so beautiful, isn't she?" He caressed a little arm, and her fingers relaxed in response.

Souls on Ice

I couldn't agree more. I took off Bobbie's sleeper so I could check out her little frame and count her tiny toes.

Relief washed over me. After being on bed rest from complications during my pregnancy, the sight of our healthy baby girl filled me with a rush of joy.

☙☙☙

Six months later, pain sent me to the doctor.

"I can't believe you carried Bobbie to term." The doctor shook his head in shock. "Your uterus is full of fibroids."

"What does that mean?" My eyes widened, taking in the news. "Can I have any more children?"

He exhaled and said, "I wouldn't recommend it. A hysterectomy is your best option."

I bit my lip, holding back the disappointment. The finality punched me in the gut. Larry was such a good father. I loved watching him cradle Bobbie in his arms and kiss her little cheeks. We wanted more children.

Back home, I fed Bobbie while I waited for Larry to get off work. I dreaded telling him the bad news.

"The doctor said I need surgery," I explained, trying to hold back the tears. "We can't have any more children."

Larry blinked back his shock. "But what about the other embryos?"

I didn't know what to say. The same worry had plagued me all afternoon.

"Are you okay?" Larry wrapped me in his arms.

The Answer

I shook my head, too overcome to speak. The unshed tears spilled down my cheeks.

"I love you," Larry whispered into my ear. "We'll make it through this. Take care of your body. What would I do without you?"

Love for this man whom I'd known for almost 20 years swelled my heart. I scheduled the dreaded hysterectomy, and he took off work for several days to take care of me and Bobbie.

❧❧❧

Because of my age, we'd opted for in vitro fertilization with Bobbie. Much to our surprise, we got pregnant the first time. Now that I could no longer carry the remaining embryos to term, Larry and I considered the dilemma facing us. The clinic sent us forms to donate the embryos for research, but neither of us felt comfortable with that option. We could donate them to an anonymous couple, but again, we didn't care for this idea, either.

I logged online and began to search other options, not sure what choices were even available. My search turned up an embryo donor and adoption program in California. Pictures of sweet babies filled the screen, while a video explained more. Peace filled me. This program gave our embryos a chance at life.

I found the contact information and gave the director a call. "You live in Washington?" she asked me after I introduced myself.

Souls on Ice

"Yes, Tacoma."

"Let me get you the number for a friend of mine." She shuffled papers in the background. "Maria Lancaster runs a similar program in Issaquah that she founded with the help of Pastor Joe Fuiten of Cedar Park Church."

I couldn't believe it. Until my research, I'd never even heard about embryo adoption, and here was an adoption center just miles down the road from us.

I hurried to call Maria, and we set up an appointment.

This was the answer.

I couldn't wait to tell Larry.

☙☙☙

Like me, Larry loved knowing our embryos would have a chance at life through adoption. Not long after our appointment with the adoption agency, we received a letter and pictures from a prospective couple named Rachel and Diony Victorin.

"Look." I pointed to a photo of them at the beach. "They like the beach, too."

Larry grinned. The beach was our favorite place in the world.

I sat down to read the letter, absorbing every word.

We have been married for seven years. We met at a wedding when Diony's best friend married Rachel's cousin. Diony is originally from Haiti and immigrated to the United States 11 years ago.

The Answer

Rachel has lived in the Seattle area her entire life. Her mom immigrated from the Netherlands when she was 9 years old. Her dad's great grandparents also immigrated from Holland, but he grew up in the Chicago area. We were both raised in Christian families and grew up in loving environments. We are still very close to both families. We call and e-mail Diony's family regularly and visit them when we can. We live close to Rachel's family, which includes her parents, two brothers and our 6-year-old nephew, Cameron. We have lunch together Sundays after church. We are especially close with Cameron and love spending time with him. Some of our favorite things to do with Cameron are playing board games, building with Legos and reading books. We also enjoy playing sports with him and going places like the zoo or the Flight Museum.

Besides spending time with our family, we also enjoy spending time together as a couple. One of our favorite things to do is to take walks on the trail near our home. The neighborhood where we live is very peaceful and safe. We also enjoy playing board games and watching family-friendly movies. We serve in our church and lead small group together.

Diony is a math teacher. His favorite things to do are pray, do math and play golf. Rachel is a pediatric nurse. She enjoys spending time with children, especially Cameron, encouraging friends, cooking and walking.

Souls on Ice

We are both Christians, and we love God with all our hearts. We live to serve him and to bring others to him. We attend a diverse, Bible-believing church that is full of life. We are leaders there and have been a part of this church for many years. The people there are very supportive and have become dear friends.

We have always loved children. Growing up, we were surrounded by siblings and cousins. Both of our careers involve working with children. After college, Diony worked with at-risk children. He has also tutored youth for many years and is now a math teacher. After high school, Rachel worked as a day camp counselor. She is now a pediatric nurse and works at a public health clinic with children from around the world.

Because of our love for children, we have always dreamed about having our own kids. We never imagined that there would be any issues with us being able to start our family. We have tried for more than three years and have gone through IVF four times. The process has been very painful, but we have grown through it, and it has helped make us who we are today. This journey has enabled us to grow in our faith and has drawn us closer to the Lord and to each other. We know that God still has children for us, even though they may come to us in a different way than we first imagined.

We first heard about embryo adoption through

The Answer

a program on Focus on the Family. We are excited about this option because it allows couples to be a part of the adopted child's life from the beginning, including pregnancy, childbirth and breastfeeding.

We are very thankful that you are giving us the gift of the opportunity to be able to have children. We are also excited to be able to give your embryos the chance of becoming the children that God has destined them to be. We believe that "children are a gift from the Lord; they are a reward from him" (Psalm 127:3), and we are so excited to become parents.

Both Rachel's brothers came to the family through adoption or foster care. Her brother Jason was adopted at birth. He didn't get to meet his birth parents until he was 30 years old. He now has a relationship with both of his birth parents and is very close to his biological mom. It has not lessened his relationship with our parents, but it has rather enhanced it.

Because we have watched the way this situation has impacted our brother and because of other reasons, we hope to have some contact with the biological family of our children. We hope to first start out having contact with your family through Cedar Park's services. We ultimately hope to have some direct contact with you in the future.

We would like the siblings to be able to know each other and to be part of each other's lives. We would also like our children to be able to know their biological parents.

*God's blessings to you,
Diony and Rachel*

As soon as I finished the last word, I knew this was the match for our embryos.

"This is the couple." I didn't hesitate in my decision. Some things a mother knows. This was one of them.

Larry's reaction mirrored mine. "She's a nurse, and he's a teacher. What better people could we find?"

In October, we met separately to sign documents releasing our embryos to Rachel and Diony. At the time, I didn't think much about the reality beyond donating our embryos. I was simply relieved to have found the perfect match for us. I never stopped to play out scenarios of *what if?*

When the e-mail arrived in February from Maria that Rachel was pregnant, a flood of emotions overwhelmed me. *This is really happening.*

"Larry," I called out to my husband, "Rachel is pregnant."

"That's awesome." He beamed. "Now what?"

I had no idea. *Would she carry the baby to term? Would we see pictures of the newborn? Would we ever meet someday in the distant future?*

Throughout the pregnancy, Rachel and I exchanged e-mails via the adoption agency.

The Answer

"Hope all is well," I wrote. "Praying for you."

Rachel's e-mails were always so grateful for the chance at motherhood.

As Rachel neared the delivery, my emotions were so high, my husband joked that I could be the one pregnant.

"Meet little Esther." Maria attached a picture in an e-mail in September. "Rachel and Diony delivered a healthy baby girl."

I stared at the sweet face and cried my head off. Esther looked so much like our Bobbie. I was ecstatic for Rachel and Diony.

"You okay, Jo?" Larry asked me.

I nodded through my tears. Joy filled my heart. We hadn't discarded this baby. Instead, we'd given her a chance at life.

���

Three months after Esther's birth, Maria sent us Christmas pictures of Esther. "Rachel really wants to meet you, Jodi."

I wasn't sure what to say. When Larry and I donated our embryos, I never expected anything beyond a few photos or notes throughout the years. I didn't want to interfere with the bonding experience between Rachel and Esther.

I tucked away the pictures and re-read another note Rachel had sent:

Souls on Ice

Dear Larry & Jodi,

Thank you so much for giving us the gift of life and our little Esther Hope! She is such a precious little girl! She loves to smile and is very sweet. Her favorite place to be is on our chest snuggling — I think she likes the warmth and the sound of our heartbeat ... When Diony and I are driving together with her in our minivan, she's happiest if she can see my face and hold my finger! It's pretty cute. She has beautiful big blue eyes and long eyelashes ... Diony and I are loving being parents! Esther smiles when she hears her daddy's voice ... even on the phone! My parents are so happy to have their first grandchild ...

How could I not agree to share our contact information? I'd text Rachel, and we could start with phone calls. Maybe we could meet later, sometime in the future.

Rachel was thrilled to get my text. She shared how much Esther was growing. Her excitement was contagious.

One afternoon while Rachel rocked Esther to sleep, I called her. Hearing her voice was almost surreal. I could hear Esther's rhythmic breathing in the background. Life was so precious, a gift so easily taken for granted.

When Rachel shared things about Esther, I couldn't get over how similar she was to Bobbie.

The Answer

"Let's do this," Rachel's voice rose in anticipation. "Let's meet somewhere."

Rachel's unselfish desire to share Esther with Larry and me overwhelmed me.

How could I not agree?

We decided on McDonald's in Federal Way, halfway between both our homes.

❧❧❧

Larry and I arrived first and let Bobbie play in the ball yard while we waited for Rachel and Esther. When Rachel maneuvered the stroller through the door, she couldn't wait to unbuckle the baby.

"Come here. Give me a hug first." I reached for a hug, feeling an instant connection. Rachel already felt like my sister.

"Do you want to hold Esther?" Rachel asked me.

I took Esther in my arms, and my heart felt like it could burst with love. "She's beautiful." Tears welled in my eyes.

No one spoke, each lost in the miracle taking place.

When my husband took Esther, his eyes twinkled with joy.

Rachel knelt down to Bobbie's level. "Do you want to hold Esther?"

Bobbie reached for Esther's hand, excited with the baby. Esther smiled, then cooed, as if trying to talk. Their obvious bond showed even at their young ages.

Souls on Ice

"This is Esther," I explained. "She's a special part of our family."

Before we left, Rachel and I promised to get the girls together again. When we embraced, I felt excited about what the future held. I was so pleased to be included in Esther's life. Gratitude overwhelmed me.

❧❧❧

Rachel loves being a mom. She calls me to compare notes between the girls or sends me notes filled with updates on Esther. In every one, she expresses her heartfelt appreciation for Esther's life.

Happy Mother's Day, Jodi! May this year be your best Mother's Day yet. Thank you so much for choosing to give Esther life and for helping to give me the gift of becoming a mother and the honor of being her mother!

Peace fills me.

The embryo contract expired after six months, but we've already promised Rachel and Diony our remaining embryo. As soon as they're ready to welcome a new baby, we'll sign the papers. I can't even imagine another family for this precious life.

At Bobbie's 4th birthday, she and Esther sat on a blanket in our backyard, totally enthralled with one another — completely oblivious to any of the other kids.

The Answer

Rachel and I watched the girls, equally mesmerized.

"It's weird how much they are alike," we echoed one another.

We laughed. We'd hung out so much, we were finishing each other's thoughts.

"I guess not, though," Rachel quickly added. "They are sisters."

Sisters.

I squeezed Rachel's hand, blessed to share the same feeling of sisterhood. "It is amazing."

જાજાજા

"How was Bobbie's first day of kindergarten?" Rachel asked me over the phone. "I took a quick break at work to let you know I'm praying for you guys today."

I covered the mouthpiece and pointed to the hall. "I'll be right outside, Bobbie. I'm talking with Aunt Rachel."

Bobbie grinned at me from the table where she sat with the other kids.

"She's doing much better now," I answered. "Bobbie had a bad dream last night that she didn't have a pet to take to show and tell. She was afraid to go to school this morning."

"Poor thing!" Rachel exclaimed. "How are you and Larry?"

"A mess. Larry's crying. I gotta be the tough one."

"I can only imagine. Esther's growing so fast, she'll be in kindergarten before long, too."

Souls on Ice

Rachel changed the subject. "So, are you ready to meet Katie Couric?"

I shook my head, still in disbelief. The talk show host wanted to interview us about embryo adoption. In less than two weeks, we would be flying to New York City with Rachel, Diony and the girls to tape our story for an audience of millions. "You know I'm a private person."

Rachel understood my concerns. If it weren't for our shared heart to let others know about embryo adoption, neither of us would agree to the attention. "Thank you for agreeing to do this."

I looked across the room full of children — lives budding with possibilities. I caught my daughter's eye and blew her a kiss. She was going to love kindergarten. One day, she'd tell her sister Esther all about it when she, too, felt nervous to start school.

Thousands of other Bobbies wait to meet sisters and brothers who have yet to be adopted.

Their stories need to be told, and we are grateful that we have been able to tell ours.

"Trust in the LORD with all your heart, and lean not on your own understanding; in all your ways acknowledge him, and he shall direct your paths." (Proverbs 3:5-6)

The Answer

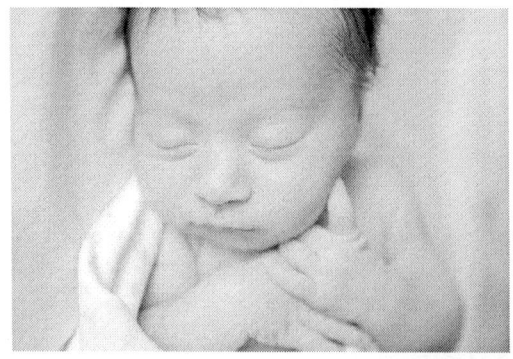

Esther Victorin as an infant

Genetic siblings Esther and Bobbie

Larry, Bobbie, Jodi, Esther, Diony and Rachel

Hope Rests
The Adoption Story of Abram and Kristin
Written by Arlene Showalter

"I wish you were mine," I whispered against the downy head in my arms. Tears rolled down my cheeks, soaking the pink receiving blanket.

Why? That single word bounced off the walls of my empty heart. *Why not me? Why not us?*

ಊಊಊ

Sophomore year, Grove City College, August 2003.
He's gorgeous, I thought, as another freshman entered the gym. I was on the Orientation Board, welcoming incoming students. We'd planned a square dance to help break the ice, and I was in charge of one square.

A pretty girl stood in my square, in need of a partner. *He's perfect for her.* I walked over to nab him for her.

"Hi," I said, "I'm Kristin. Welcome to GCC." I gestured to my incomplete square. "We need you."

"Abram." He grinned and trotted after me.

Shortly after that, Abram stopped to chat with me between classes.

He's so nice. He even remembers my name.

These impromptu chats continued until one day when he walked up while I was talking to my friend, another curly red-haired girl named Kristin. He looked at me, then Other Kristin and back.

Abram's face reddened.

He thought we were the same girl. I smothered a laugh.

Because GCC is a small college, we ran into one another often. We attended the same Bible study at our pastor's home and walked back to our dorms together. Abram and his guitar joined a school worship team on which I played keyboard.

We began dating the following year. During my senior year, Abram handed me a paper.

"What's this?" I asked.

His brown eyes danced. "Read and follow," he said.

I unfolded the paper. It was a clue. It led me through a treasure hunt all over the campus. As I located each clue, a note and rose waited. *Here's where we shared our first kiss*, one read, then provided the hint for the next location.

The final clue instructed me to dress for a hike. I hurried to comply.

"Ready?" Abram asked when I met him at the dorm entrance. He took my hand and led me toward a waterfall he had discovered weeks earlier. A shiver went up my spine when I heard the rushing waters. *I've always dreamed of being kissed behind a waterfall.* It glowed in the approaching darkness from dozens of luminaries placed around the area.

Abram pulled out the words to a song he had written for me months before, changing the words to suit his goal.

Hope Rests

"Will you be my wife? Are you ready for this?"

I grinned. "I'm ready!"

He took my hand and drew me behind the falls. There lay a huge boulder with the words *Kristin, will you marry me?* carved into its surface. Candles on top illuminated roses and a sparkling engagement ring.

I turned to look at Abram. There he knelt in the mud, wide grin splitting his face.

"Will you marry me?" he asked.

"Of course!" I answered.

He took me in his arms and kissed me there, behind the falls. The rushing waters drowned the pounding of my heart.

Afterward, Abram took me out for a romantic dinner. When I returned to my dorm, heart-shaped balloons filled the room, all proclaiming, *I love you!*

I sank down on my bed. The declarations I'd made to friends long ago echoed in my head. *I'm going to marry a man 6 feet tall, with brown eyes and hair, good teeth, dimples and broad shoulders,* I'd stated with all the confidence of a 12 year old.

"Oh, my gosh," I gasped. "Abram is all that *and more.*"

ช่ช่ช่

Plans I'd laid with precision began happening.

First: Get a degree in Elementary and Early Childhood Education. Check.

Second: Marry the man of my dreams. Check.

Souls on Ice

Third: Teach three years.
Fourth: Start a family at age 25.
Fifth: Have a baby every two years until family consists of five children.

I moved back to the State of Washington and secured a job, teaching fourth grade. Abram stayed in Pennsylvania for his senior year. Letters filled the empty hours. We grew closer in heart through the long separation.

After being reunited in marriage, in July 2007, Abram moved to Washington and secured a job. Expected events hummed along like a well-oiled machine.

I quit teaching after my third year, as planned, hoping that our fourth goal of starting a family lay a mere nine months or so away.

Summer came and went. No pregnancy.

I returned to the school as a volunteer, to fill the empty days, but it seemed every face held the same question. *Aren't you supposed to be pregnant?*

I quit volunteering to avoid the unasked questions.

Dad and I stood chatting in his kitchen.

"You hear the news?"

"What news?" I asked.

"Erica's pregnant."

My heart dropped. *Why? Why?* My head throbbed with the endless question. My sister-in-law had recently married and wasn't even trying to have a baby.

Hope Rests

What's wrong with me? Where are you, God?

❧❧❧

"Why not just cut to the chase and find a fertility specialist?" my friend Laura suggested. "You might regret it if you keep waiting."

I hesitated. *What if they find I'm not whole? But Laura's right. I'm accomplishing nothing by waiting.*

I first made calls to regular obstetricians, hearing the same responses over and over. "How long have you been trying to get pregnant?" Long silences always followed my answer before the next predictable reply: "You're young. What's the hurry?"

I finally made it in to see a doctor.

"How long have you been trying to get pregnant?" she asked.

"Six months."

She peered at me over her eyeglasses.

"Six months," she repeated, disdain coloring her words. Her eyes flicked over my information.

"Well," I started. "I've always had an irregular cycle, so I thought perhaps I may have problems."

She glanced at the chart again. "Says you have heart issues." Her manner turned accusatory.

"No," I said. "I've been checked."

"How can you be so irresponsible," she said, ignoring my last statement, "wanting to bring a child into the world with the possibility of heart problems? And …" Her annoyance deepened, "six months and you're already worried?"

I fled from her presence, confused. Dazed. "You're young. What's the hurry?" Her words taunted me.

All my carefully laid plans crumbled to dust in my heart. *Maybe I need to back off and relax.*

One year later, in August of 2010, Dr. L, a fertility specialist, agreed to see me. Hope revived.

"We'll schedule an ultrasound," Dr. L said, "to make sure you're ovulating."

The test came back negative.

"We'll run another test to make sure your fallopian tubes aren't blocked."

I lay through the excruciating pain of the procedure, reminding myself, *It's all worth it.*

"Your tubes are fine," Dr. L said, "so we'll proceed with drugs to get you ovulating." He grinned. "I predict you'll be pregnant within six months." The grin widened. "I love getting 26 year olds pregnant."

"This is it!" I told Abram later, my heart soaring. "By this time next year, we could have our very own baby!"

છે છે છે

November 2010

I'm looking outside at our trees with fall colors as I type. The wind picks up the fallen leaves and whirls them around, over and over again. Right when they settle to the

Hope Rests

ground again, they are picked up by another sudden gust, never to rest. It reminds me of the hopes of a woman trying to conceive. Every month they are picked up and whirled around by different positive or negative symptoms, tests and procedures. They often get lifted, oh so high, and then eventually dropped again to an even greater depth. But that dropping of hope is temporary, until they are picked up again the next month, whirled around and then dropped again with the beginning of each new cycle.

Three months passed. Tests proved I was ovulating. Hope soared.

"Nothing," I sighed to Abram. "I don't understand why I'm not pregnant."

We returned to Dr. L.

"You can try IUIs," he suggested. "Intrauterine insemination."

"What is that?" I asked, "and what are the chances of success?"

"Sperm is injected directly into your womb when we know you are ovulating," he said. "Success rate is around 15 percent."

Abram raised his eyebrows.

"Any chance is worth it," I said. "Let's do it. God's in control and with us, no matter what happens."

My heart thumped as a nurse performed the procedure. *This is it, this is it,* it seemed to say.

The results came in. Failure to Conceive.

Souls on Ice

❧❧❧

"Meet your Auntie Kristin," my brother Josh said, as he laid his daughter in my arms. I held her close, breathing the smell of newborn Everly. Sobs choked me as I closed my eyes to everyone around me. *I wish you were mine,* I thought. *This is the moment I've dreamed and prayed for all my life.*

I felt Everly's soft breath against my damp cheek. *You feel so right in my arms. But you're not mine.* My breath caught. *I have to give you back.*

I felt gentle hands brushing my arms and opened my eyes. Abram bent close, willing comfort and strength through his deep brown eyes. He lifted Everly from me and cuddled her close.

I watched my perfect, whole husband caress his tiny niece and examine every perfect, whole finger and toe. My entire being ached — spirit, soul and body. *Infertile. Half a woman. Imperfect.*

❧❧❧

We tried IUI a second time. And a third. And fourth. The results stayed the same: Failure to Conceive.

May 2011

I only have two tries left of this procedure I've been undergoing ... The sun is shining on the trees outside. I know it to be true. Though when I look out the window, I only see rain. My husband kisses my forehead and pulls

Hope Rests

me close to him. I know it's happening. But I feel nothing. Only tears welling in my eyes and streaking mascara down my face. Just ugliness. He says, "I'm sorry." But I'm sorry. I've failed again. I didn't eat right, I exercised too much and I let my hopes soar. Birds are chirping and lawn mowers are running, a sure sign of spring and new life. But there is no life. No child, no new soul, no first coos and giggles or sleepless nights to look forward to. No hugs or roses on Mother's Day. My womb is empty. Within the next couple of days I will feel pain and lose whatever ugliness there is in there. Where is joy? I have none. Where is God in this?

Fifth procedure. Failure.

Sixth attempt. In the deepest depth of my being, I thought that God would answer our prayers. *This is the right time. We'll have our own flesh-and-blood baby in our arms this time next year.*

The procedure mirrored the previous five. Failure.

We stared at Dr. L. *What next?* Our eyes begged.

"Have you considered in vitro fertilization?" he asked.

"What all is involved?" Abram's voice remained calm, as though he already knew the answer.

"Eggs are extracted from Kristin," he said. "We normally take up to 30 to ensure the best results. After fertilizing them with Abram's sperm, we allow them to grow and then examine the results."

"What are you looking for?"

Souls on Ice

"We look to find the most promising ones. We call those *viable*. We'll take the best looking two or three that have survived and implant them into Kristin's womb. The rest we can freeze for later. You won't have 30 embryos at this point. Many eggs won't get fertilized, and some embryos won't make it through the entire process."

"What do you do with the embryos that don't look promising?" I asked. "The *non*-viable?"

"It is up to you," he said, "but we can throw those away. And the embryos you don't use can also be discarded, or given over to scientific research, or frozen indefinitely."

I knew Abram had serious reservations about IVF since he knew we were discussing the future of possibly 30 souls. I wasn't sure if it was ethical or not, but if it meant having my husband's child, I'd go for it.

"We'll have to discuss it." Abram stood. I followed. Despair wrapped icy fingers around my heart — and squeezed.

"Glad you could come for dinner," I said to Stacy, my dearest friend since high school. She and I had both endured the frustration and pain of infertility. We shared our hopes and disappointments on a regular basis. I held open the door as she and her husband, Tom, came inside. Their toddler, Haly, shuffled in behind them, peering at me from behind her mom's legs. My eyes followed Haly's every movement from prancing around the living room to dropping her sippy cup during the meal. Stacy and Tom had gone through the process of embryo adoption to have Haly.

Embryo adoption? I thought, studying Haly. *Fine for you, but it just seems a little weird. Besides, I've washed my hands of getting pregnant. I'm done. Exhausted.*

"It's not a bad option," Tom said, when the conversation turned to the same subject.

"I've always been open to adoption," Abram said. He turned to me. "Maybe we should research this." His eyes caught mine and held. "Why go for IVF with its ethical dilemmas when we have the opportunity to adopt ones already created?"

I hesitated. I wanted Abram's baby, complete with his eyes, hair and dimples. Not a child created by someone else.

"Think about it," Tom said. "God is perfect and his Son, Jesus, perfect, too. But because of what Jesus did on the cross at Calvary, God willingly adopts us, imperfect sinners, into his family. We are his full sons and daughters and are not only forgiven, but we receive an inheritance in heaven as a true child would."

My mind flew back to what I'd read before in Galatians 4:4-7:

"But when the fullness of time had come, God sent forth his Son, born of woman, born under the law, to redeem those who were under the law, so that we might receive *adoption as sons.* And because you are sons, God has sent the Spirit of his Son into our hearts, crying, 'Abba! Father!' So you are no longer a slave [to the law], but a son, and if a son, then an heir through God" (English Standard Version, italics added).

It hit me. *If God did it for me, then why am I struggling to do it for someone else?*

I want to go for embryo adoption, I thought to myself the next morning.

I e-mailed Abram at work. He immediately gave me the go-ahead.

I e-mailed Stacy. "Okay," I said, "I'm ready to do it. What do I do? Whom do I call?"

"Maria," she wrote back. "I'll give you her e-mail address. She coordinates embryo adoptions."

My name is Kristin, I typed. *My husband, Abram, and I are interested in embryo adoption.* I pressed the send button.

September 2011

Lately, I haven't been able to get the term "adoption" out of my head ... Well, I can't claim that this means God's will is for me to adopt, but perhaps it was in his will that the idea of adoption has clamped tighter than a pit bull's jaws onto my mind.

Two years and six months to the day [we started trying to have a family] — that was the day adoption became clear to me and was no longer simply a drudging last resort. That was the day the word "adoption" was accompanied by the word "joy."

Hope Rests

Maria sent an application. I sped through the reams of paperwork and sent it back.

I'm going to be a mom, I scribbled on a church bulletin during service and shoved it under my mother's nose. Now that I'd embraced adoption, I knew that somehow, someway, God would answer my prayers. I no longer questioned his method.

"What are you doing?" Abram asked, a few weeks later, when he discovered me cleaning every inch of our home.

"The social worker is coming for a home study," I said.

"I think they just want to see how we live," Abram said.

"But so much depends on this," I said, turning back to my scrub brush.

"We'll pass." His gentle laugh calmed me — a little.

I was upstairs when Abram answered the door. "Hello, my name is Heather," the pleasant-faced lady told him. "I'm here to do your home study."

I hurried downstairs as Abram led the woman who held our future in her hands to our dining room.

Moments after taking our seats, Pip, our kitty, leapt up from the back of Heather's chair and attached himself to her back.

Oh, no! My heart stopped. *She'll flunk us for safety issues.*

Heather laughed as Abram peeled Pip off her. I relaxed — somewhat.

Souls on Ice

She asked probing questions — *How much money do you make? How do you resolve conflicts between you? How were you raised, and how do you plan to raise your own children?* — but her friendliness and professionalism helped. She passed us, Pip's claws notwithstanding, and we moved on to the next step.

We were instructed to write a letter of introduction to prospective donor families and create a photo book, along with more paperwork.

I took the massive envelope to the local post office on November 16, 2011.

"You want to send this priority?" the clerk asked.

I hesitated. My whole life and dreams lay in that packet, to be accepted or rejected by some nameless, unknown donor family.

"What is your slowest rate?" I asked.

He named it, surprise etched across his face.

"I'll take it," I said.

"Okay."

We met Maria in person the following month.

"Please, come in," she said as we entered her office. "Sit down."

We took the two chairs facing her desk.

"First," she said, "let me congratulate you on your progress thus far."

She motioned to a framed photo of a child. "My own success story with embryo adoption."

We examined the picture.

Hope Rests

"You see," she said, "this isn't just a job for me. It's a passion. I pray over every prospective adoption, every match. I believe in the God of miracles and that he means for a certain embryo to go to a certain family. I'm not placing a mass of cells. I'm placing a soul, a living human being."

We nodded. "That's why we were hesitant to do IVF," Abram said. "We struggled with the ethical questions it raised."

"Exactly," Maria agreed. "We treat this process like a conventional adoption, even though it is pre-birth and not post."

In February 2012, Maria sent us an e-mail confirming that she had sent our packet of information to a potential donor family. All that was left to do was wait and pray.

I waited an agonizing month with no news. *Have they heard from the donor family? Have they accepted us?*

Abram and I went to Cannon Beach, Oregon, the first weekend in March, returning late Monday night. Early the next morning, before he'd awakened, I got up and flipped on the computer and clicked into my e-mail. There sat a message from Maria. My finger trembled as I pressed *open.*

The family says yes.

The family says yes. I read the words again. Gradually, comprehension dawned. The donor family said YES! I started jumping up and down and raced to our bedroom where Abram slept, oblivious to the news.

Souls on Ice

"They said yes, they said yes!" I yelled, bouncing on the bed.

Abram struggled awake, eyeing his apparently crazy wife through sleepy eyes.

"They said yes," I repeated. "We're parents!"

Abram stretched and rubbed his eyes. "I wonder what our kids will look like."

I threw my arms wide. "Thank you, God, for such a joyous day!"

We received a packet of information about our donor family and learned they had only two embryos to offer. Since the success rate of embryo implantation rests at about 35 percent, most couples hope to adopt more to ensure pregnancy.

"We have to give those two little guys a chance at life," Abram said. "Let's go for it."

After three months of legal work, transferring ownership of the embryos to us, medical exams and taking hormones to prepare my body for pregnancy, the day arrived.

I chose my outfit with great care. *Today, I meet my children for the first time.* Afterward, I sat down to write a letter to my children:

June 5, 2012

We were called back. The room was much nicer than my normal room. Soft white sheets lined the patient bed.

Hope Rests

A curtain blocked the door. It was quiet, spacious and private. The nurse gave me a few instructions and then left. I got ready.

Soon, the friendly embryologist entered the room. He handed us a photo, and we gasped. It was our first photo of you. You both were the most beautiful things we had ever seen! It was difficult to take our eyes off of you two. Somehow, seeing your photo made me feel like I had met you, and it was then that my heart was filled to overflowing with love for you.

The embryologist told us how healthy you looked, explaining how you had contracted with being frozen, but that you both should expand within eight hours. He then went on to explain how the procedure would take place, how he'd put you two in a little tube, hand you to Dr. K, Dr. K would carefully place you inside my womb and he'd double check to make sure both of you were no longer in the tube. He'd flush it out, and silly me, I said, "You'll have something underneath to catch them with, right?" He assured me he would.

He left, and Dr. K and the nurse came in. Both of them were friendly, almost joyous. They and the embryologist seemed excited, like Daddy and I were.

Dr. K did a practice run that Daddy videotaped. Then she waited at the window for you two to be handed over to her. The screen above her head flicked on, and Daddy and I saw our last name flash across the screen. The label was taken away, and we realized we were looking into the bottom of a Petri dish. As we were figuring out what we

Souls on Ice

were looking at, the microscopic camera zoomed in, and your two cheery round selves came into view, nice and clear.

Shortly after you appeared on the screen, the tip of a tube came into view, and we could see your two little forms being taken away — hopefully to be seen again this side of glory! What an amazing sight it was!

The embryologist carefully handed you two over to Dr. K. She then took you over to me. I focused on your photo and kissed it, and then I held it to my chest.

The screen switched over to the ultrasound image that the nurse was projecting. We could see the white line of the tube as Dr. K carefully placed you two in just the right spot. She very carefully withdrew the tube, handing it to the embryologist to double check that you two were safe inside me, and she started to put away her contraptions. I asked her if you both had made it out of the tube, and she said yes. She set a little timer for 15 minutes and left us.

After a couple of minutes, I ran to the restroom, then I came back to lie down and marvel with Abram at what we had all just experienced. I now had two tiny precious lives fighting to survive inside of me.

I knew then that I loved you and that my love had no bounds. You were mine. My children, my babies, my life, my everything. More precious to me than I ever could have imagined.

Seeing you two before my very eyes — words cannot begin to describe the sense of awe that filled my being. This transfer — from a cold, sterile room to a warm, living

Hope Rests

womb — was amazing. The science, the hand of God, the preciousness of life — my mind was full to bursting with trying to fathom what was taking place even now!

Abram had brought to my mind that morning Psalm 139. It became our meditation that day, June 5, 2012.

The gravity of your situation and ours ... it is heavy, but surreal. We continue to pray that God will preserve your lives and save your souls.

We waited nine excruciating days before I could take the pregnancy test. I sobbed while a lab technician drew my blood. *I just know we're doomed for another disappointment.* Every nerve in my body felt like a live wire.

Mom drove me home and dropped me off. Then I waited ... and waited ... for *the call.* It came several hours later.

I can't face this alone. I let it go to voicemail and sent Abram a text. *Got the call.*

Moments later, he called, his breath in bunches as he sprinted for his car. "I was in a meeting," he said, "so I told them I had a family emergency. See you in a few."

"Should we record this?" I asked, as Abram burst through the door.

"Sure," he said, then hesitated. "We can always erase it, if it's bad news."

He set up the video camera while I hovered nearby. We prayed together, to collect our senses, then he pressed the record button on the camera and nodded.

I dialed my voicemail. A voice came over the speakerphone, calm and measured. "The results are in …"

"It's negative." I looked at Abram, shaking my head.

"… I'm happy to report they came back positive."

Positive? Shock claimed me. *I'm pregnant? Surely I heard the message wrong.* Understanding eluded us.

My jaw dropped the same time Abram laid his head on the table. I pressed the button to listen again.

"… happy to report they came back positive."

We hugged. We kissed. We shouted. "We're pregnant!"

After calling Abram's parents in New Jersey with our happy news, we drove over to my parents' home. Mom stood at the window, looking out, as we screeched to a halt in their driveway.

"I'm pregnant!" I said, the moment she flung the door open. She staggered back and then caught herself. Tears and hugs and more phone calls filled the rest of the day.

A month later, Dr. L performed an ultrasound to determine whether or not we'd be having twins. He found one heartbeat. "Are you sure there's only one?" we asked.

The doctor was sure. We felt sorrow for our loss, but also rejoiced in the fact that the other baby was definitely alive and growing inside me.

We chose to have a natural husband-coached water birth for our baby. In this style, the mother sits, immersed to her waist, in warm water. The father positions himself beside her as her doula, or labor coach. My hubby, who'd traveled the long, stark and cheerless road of infertility with me, now jumped into both tub and event, eager to experience as much hands-on as possible.

The moment after the final, painful push, the midwife laid our baby on my chest. I gazed at this miracle, this perfect human being lying against me.

I rubbed his tiny back, and he cried. I touched his chubby limbs, his cheeks, his head. My son. My perfect, beautiful son. So alive. So mine.

Abram leaned forward for a kiss. Our first as parents of our born son. He cut the cord and held our new son tight against his chest.

March 2013

My sweet Asher,

Welcome to the world! I just put you down for a nap, and I already cannot wait to see you again! Daddy and I love studying everything about you: your soft, sweet-smelling skin, your fuzzy head, your kissable chubby cheeks, your pouty lips, your calm, clear eyes, your perfect nose, your gentle fingers and tiny toes, your little tummy and I could go on filling pages and pages! I'm trying desperately to capture pictures of all of your expressions and videos of all your little noises ... I don't want to forget anything about my darling baby.

You are such a sweet baby. You are calm and mellow, and you have enjoyed opening your eyes and staring into mine since the beginning! You know just what to do to melt my heart. I'm looking forward to filling this book with memories of you and your childhood! You are my sweetest gift — my heart overflows with love for you, dear Asher!

The moment you were born was the most incredible moment of my life. I can still feel your little limbs pressed against my chest, and my lips can still feel your wet, smooth head and face. You took a moment to breathe. They had me hold, caress and talk to you. You started a gurgly cry, so Daddy and I sang "Baby Mine" to you. I remember crying out, "My baby!" and "He's real!" That's what struck me just at that moment. You were real! Little, complete you! And you had a soul! And you were our son. Our son, the one we had longed for, cried over and prayed for. Our greatest gift! It was so hard to hand you over to Daddy after he cut the cord. I was, and am, so in love, so enamored with you, my little Asher. You surely have my heart. I love you more than I ever dreamed it was possible to love a child. You are my sweet boy.

Love, Mommy

ॐॐॐ

I took Asher to the grocery store a few weeks later.

"He's so cute," the cashier said as I checked out. "You think he'll have your red hair?"

"I gave birth to him," I said, hiding a smile, "but, actually, he's adopted."

She stared like a deer in headlights. The cashier at the next register leaned over the divider, frowning.

"Say what?" she asked.

I laughed and began explaining embryo adoption.

My cashier's eyes misted. "I've been trying to get pregnant for several years."

I gave her what information I could and left, Asher tucked firmly in my arms.

Thank you, God, for the opportunity to spread the word about embryo adoption!

I love to converse with people who saw me before Asher's birth and I tell them he's adopted. Blank looks always follow that statement. I can see the wheels turning in their heads, like they're thinking, *But I saw you pregnant!*

These incidences open up conversations to prove that life truly begins at conception. Others get an "aha" moment and say, "Oh, so you're like a surrogate mother!"

"Yes," I reply, always with a smile, "except I get to keep my baby."

I cuddle my son, my perfect Asher, and my heart swells in love and appreciation.

Thank you, God, for my infertility. I know now that if I hadn't struggled, I wouldn't have had Asher, and Asher is who I wanted all along.

Souls on Ice

Dedicated to my son, Asher:

As I write you will be born,
In just a few weeks' time.
No longer do I wait and mourn,
For a sweet baby mine.

Your mommy and daddy, we loved each other so,
But try as we might, no tiny flower would grow.
We cried, and we prayed, and we cried a little more,
But for us it seemed no baby was in store.

We went to the doctor, but the doctor shook his head,
We came home wondering if our dream was really dead.
Please, a child to hold, a little one to love!
God also said, "No," though He knew what we dreamed of.

Give up, we did not, and you know that full well,
God answered our prayer, though at first we couldn't tell.
Our bodies not working was a blessing, you see,
If they worked naturally, you wouldn't be here with me.

So special, you were chosen,
My child, we adopted you,
A flower, yes, once frozen,
You and another, too!

You already had life, you know,
But your heart didn't beat,
You had a soul — we knew it, though,
We both had yet to meet.

Hope Rests

The months, they came and went so fast,
We found out you were a boy,
Just a few more months to pass,
Then we'd hold this bundle of joy!

Our God has been so good to us,
He showed us where to walk,
The path has been adventurous,
But He has been our rock.

You have a story of adoption,
Yes, my dear, that's true,
God chose for us the greatest option,
That was adopting you.

But did you know, my baby dear,
We are adopted, too?
Daddy and I, we'd like to clear
A detail, one or two.

God sent His only Son to die,
For the sins of Daddy and me,
Because no matter how we'd try,
We couldn't live perfectly.

So Jesus took away our sin,
He died instead of us,
God sees us not as we have been,
He sees us through the cross.

When we trust upon His name,
He takes us in His hand,

Souls on Ice

He makes us nevermore the same,
By grace alone we stand.

He loves us as His children,
Our Father, He becomes,
Forgives us of our sin,
We're now His little ones.

So chosen, we were, too,
Just like we chose sweet you,
We hope someday you'll know,
That Jesus loves you so.

"But when the fullness of time had come, God sent forth his Son, born of woman, born under the law, to redeem those who were under the law, so that we might receive *adoption as sons*. And because you are sons, God has sent the Spirit of his Son into our hearts, crying, 'Abba! Father!' So you are no longer a slave [to the law], but a son, and if a son, then an heir through God." (Galatians 4:4-7 ESV)

Hope Rests

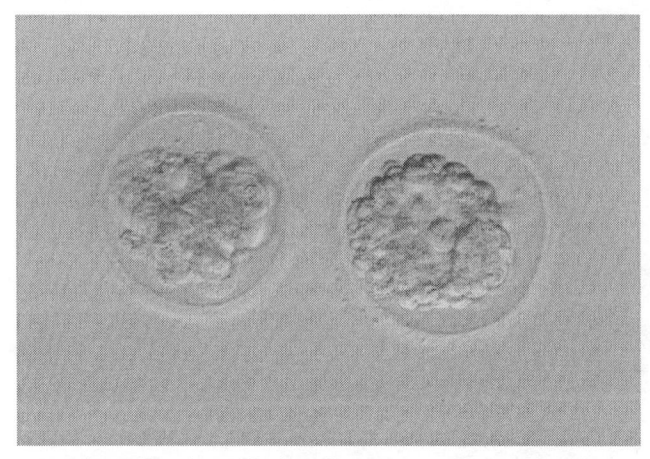

Two thawed embryos before they were transferred to Kristin's womb

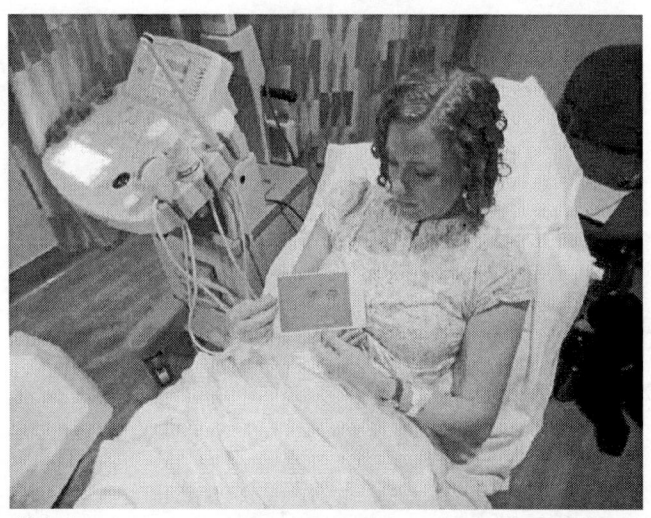

Kristin

Souls on Ice

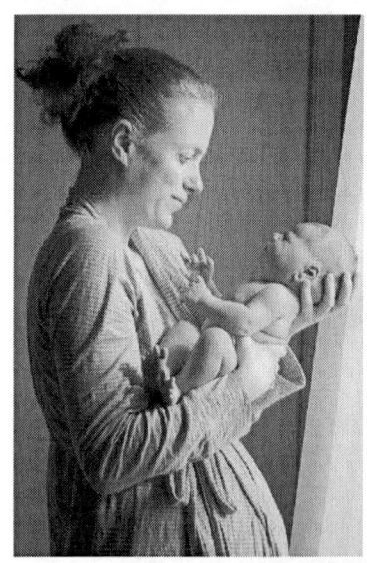

Kristin and Asher

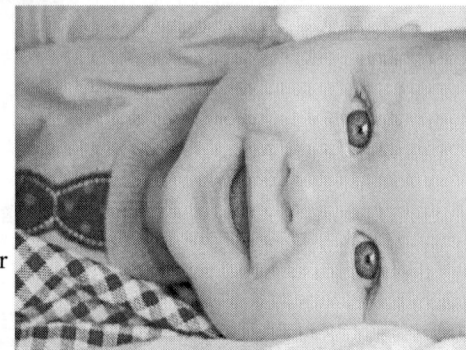

Asher

Kristin, Asher and Abram

Babies Everywhere!
The Adoption Story of Daniel and Zoe
Written by Marty Minchin

The crosswalk light on Michigan Avenue indicated it was safe to proceed, but instead of walking ahead, I swiveled to stare at the situation unfolding beside me. A rumpled, unkempt mom screamed at a little boy, berating him for some minor infraction. With her baby parked next to her in its stroller, she focused on her toddler, smacking him loudly while he cried.

The boy's hysterical wails escalated above his mother's yells, and I wondered if there was anything such a small child could have done to deserve such an embarrassingly loud and public takedown.

I glanced down at my smart high heels and business suit and smoothed my hair. *I would never be that kind of mom. She should hold his hand, not hit him.*

I sidled over until I was so close I could touch the child. My appearance was that of a put-together businesswoman, but inside I was torn to pieces. Daniel and I had been trying, to no avail, to have a child for several years. The lessons I'd learned in the world of finance — that the amount of effort you put into something directly affects the outcome — didn't apply in the world of infertility. The money, time, work and emotion we'd poured into trying to have a baby had come up nil.

Why is it that this is the one thing every woman is supposed to be able to do, and I'm not succeeding?

It would have been so easy for me to grab the boy's arm and walk away with him. I'm not even sure if the mom would have objected.

The next time the traffic light turned green, I crossed the street — alone. I don't steal children, but desperation can lead the mind to crazy places.

☙☙☙

Daniel and I met the day our best friends married each other, where I was the maid of honor and he was the best man. He lived in Toronto, and I lived in Chicago. After two years of dating long distance, he moved to Chicago so we could start our lives together. Our plan was to enjoy a year or two of married life and then begin our family. We were athletes with good careers, and we assumed that enlarging our family was a natural next step.

At first, the prospect of infertility didn't even occur to us. With our lax use of birth control, I should have gotten pregnant the day we were married. When we started consciously trying for a baby several years later, it just didn't seem to work. But I was young — only 29 — and I wasn't too worried about our ultimate chances for success when I started fertility treatments.

We jumped right in. I met with three reproductive

Babies Everywhere!

endocrinologists, took Clomid and endured a battery of tests. Doctors promised us that in vitro fertilization would work, but after three painful IVFs, I produced only one embryo. Two of the procedures were cancelled due to "poor stimulation."

Undeterred, I made trying to get pregnant a lifestyle. I tried prayer, acupuncture, meditation and massage. To stay active, I played and taught tennis. I forced myself to keep a positive outlook. Daniel and I took a relaxing vacation to Costa Rica and hung out in a rainforest. When a Chinese doctor advised herbal tea, I drank every variety he suggested. If anyone who had successfully gotten pregnant after struggling with infertility offered me advice, I followed it to the letter.

While my womb remained empty, the world around me seemed to fill with babies. Every woman I passed on the streets of Chicago was either pregnant or cradling a newborn. My friends began to get pregnant, and I pasted a smile on my face as I attended baby shower after baby shower. Friends who had never liked children seemed to be popping them out right and left.

On paper, Daniel and I were ideal parents. We loved kids. We had a slew of nieces and nephews between us, and we regularly had several of them over at a time to spend the night. We took them swimming and ice skating. We knew how to change diapers. I had worked as a teacher early in my career.

But for us, six years of trying only produced one failure after another.

Souls on Ice

When I was 32, a doctor told me that we should call it quits. Conceiving was not in our future. The doctor concluded that my husband's sperm was not working well, and my body acted like that of a 57 year old. I didn't have many eggs, and the ones I did have were of poor quality.

A period of mourning set in. We mourned the children we would never have, the sons and daughters who would never have my hair and Daniel's sense of humor. As the little hands we dreamed of holding slowly slipped out of our grasp, we retreated into hiding. Once the last ones to leave the dance floor at a party, Daniel and I became no-shows at family events. We skipped my aunt's 50th birthday party because I couldn't handle any more questions about when we were going to have children. Broken, I stayed at home and cried, engulfed in stress and sadness.

Determined to be a mom, I found another equally difficult path to walk — traditional adoption. I wanted a child in our lives, no matter how he or she might get there. Our adoption counselor advised us that we were "jumping from one frying pan into another," but I approached adoption with the same zest I had fertility treatments. I dragged Daniel to two adoption conferences and patiently worked through a lengthy home study to prove that we would be fit parents. With our paperwork processed, all we had to do was wait and hope that our hearts wouldn't completely break in the meantime.

☙☙☙

Babies Everywhere!

If I had known my boss' wife, Melanie, had been pregnant, I never would have accepted their invitation to join them for dinner in downtown Chicago. I had become so depressed about my own lack of children that I couldn't stand to be around new parents or about-to-be parents. One of my dearest friends suffered from postpartum depression after having her baby, and it was a struggle for me to drive to her house to support her. In the end, I couldn't be the friend she needed.

Melanie didn't look pregnant in the dress she was wearing, so when Daniel and I sat down with them, we carried on conversation as normal.

Something in Melanie's eyes, though, connected with the sadness in mine. I found myself opening up to her, even though we hardly knew each other. When I brought up our long struggle with infertility, Melanie told us about hers. We had surprisingly similar pasts. Melanie had also produced only a single embryo in three IVF attempts. But when she told me she was newly pregnant, the familiar anger flared over the ongoing injustice that seemingly every woman in the world could get pregnant but me.

Then, Melanie dropped a phrase that reignited the hope in my heart.

Embryo adoption.

Melanie was the first client to work with Maria Lancaster, director of Embryo Adoption Services of Cedar Park. I had every faith that my boss and his wife researched every aspect of Maria's organization. We worked at a prominent investment firm where we spent our days evaluating the merits of other organizations as potential investments — our professional lives were based on making sound choices. I hesitantly allowed my brain to wander: *Could this work for us as well? Could this dinner conversation be God showing us our path to parenthood?*

The light from my computer screen flickered long into the night after Daniel and I got home from dinner. I typed "embryo adoption" into Google and read all about Maria's mission to give embryos created through IVF a chance to be born. Her Web site described embryos as "a precious gift of matchless value" and "a human being at its earliest stages."

As I read, the glimmer of hope grew. Because Daniel had never fully bought into traditional adoption, he surprised me when he quickly agreed to pursuing embryo adoption.

Maybe, just maybe, Daniel and I would become parents.

❧❧❧

Within a few minutes of talking to Maria the next morning, I felt like I had known her my entire life. I had come to believe that even the most skilled doctors couldn't assure us of anything — at best, pregnancy felt more like gambling. Science and medicine had failed us, and as Maria told me about her passion for life and her vision for connecting all frozen embryos with loving families, my heart swelled. This was the right fit for us. We had to place

Babies Everywhere!

our hope in God, and Maria felt like an answer to our prayers.

Traditional adoption never felt hopeful, as counselors and agencies repeatedly reminded us that the process could take a long time, and in the end, we might never be matched with a child. Maria's warmth traveled over the phone lines, and I quickly felt like I was talking with a family member who genuinely cared about our situation. She became a living angel to us, someone who would guide us on a new journey where the ending seemed hopeful.

Daniel and I filled out our embryo adoption applications and mailed them to Maria. The extensive home study we completed for traditional adoption, which had taken nine months, was more than adequate for Maria's requirements, and we were fast-tracked for approval.

Then, I sat down to make a scrapbook about our lives for potential embryo donors. We had to present ourselves through words and pictures, showing embryo donors why we wanted a child and what that child's life would be like with us.

"Welcome to Daniel and Zoe's photo collage," I began. "Thank you for taking the time to look through our photo book. We have faith that one day we will be blessed with a child, and we hope this book brings us a little closer to that day."

I chose pictures carefully, scrutinizing each one to make sure it best represented our life. I began with

Souls on Ice

pictures of the day Daniel and I met, followed by pictures of things we had done together. Scuba diving, rock climbing, skiing, traveling and standing in front of the Grand Canyon. I wanted the family to see that our lives were filled with love and laughter.

I added pictures of our large extended families, who we see often. I filled pages with pictures of Daniel and me taking our nephews and nieces to museums, playing sports, building sandcastles and reading with them. Next came photos of us with our friends, playing tennis, hanging out, snowboarding and competing in triathlons.

"We look forward to all of the possibilities of our future years," I concluded at the end of the book. "Thank you again for your consideration."

I closed the cover, terrified. Did I put the right pictures in? Did I present myself well? Are they going to like me? When I dropped it in the mail, I felt like I was sitting on the side of the school gymnasium, waiting for someone to ask me to dance. As the days went by and we anxiously waited, it seemed like we would never get picked. I prayed that someone would read the book and want us to become parents to their embryos.

❧❧❧

The e-mail came a month and a half later while I was at work. A family was interested in us!

I printed out the message, grabbed my friend Laura and rushed her to the library in our office. We cried

Babies Everywhere!

together as I read the e-mail over and over, and then I called Daniel to tell him the good news. I was filled with excitement, but I forced myself to keep my emotions in check. I didn't want to fully get my hopes up, only to have the rug pulled out from under me again if this attempt at pregnancy didn't work. Infertility piles sadness on top of sadness.

When the potential embryo donors' paperwork arrived, we couldn't believe the similarities to our story. Daniel and I sat on the couch and pored over the three letters and pictures of their three children jumping ropes, making crafts and hiking.

This couple also struggled to conceive, but unlike me, the mom had endured several miscarriages. After learning that the mom carried a gene that caused her to miscarry, her sister donated eggs to create the embryos. I was overwhelmed with this woman's act of generosity to help her sister have a baby.

Daniel and I cried as we read her words, connecting with the heartbreak we knew all too well. This family was so much like us. They had a similar financial background, and the mom came from a large family like mine. We even shared a strong faith in God. Maria works to pair donor and adoption families with similar characteristics, and Daniel and I quickly decided this was a match.

We also were drawn to what the family had written about embryo adoption.

We firmly believe that all embryos have the potential for life and therefore need to be treated with respect and

Souls on Ice

dignity and not just discarded after we felt our family was complete. We believe that this potential for life is a gift from God and should be treated as such; therefore, we would never allow our embryos to be used for scientific research purposes.

Being a planner, I always had a backup strategy when trying for a baby. This time, I literally decided to put all of my eggs in one basket. Maria completed our match with the donor family, who gave us all seven of their frozen embryos. We were skeptical because the embryos had been frozen for 10 years, and we knew that shipping the embryos to Chicago could be tricky. The microscopic embryos arrived frozen in four tiny straws: We decided to unfreeze three embryos of the seven that we adopted.

The multitude of tests I had over the years finally paid off. My doctor didn't need further information to affirm that I was physically able to carry a baby to term. My problem had always been with the quality and amount of my eggs, rather than the health of my body.

The prep work for embryo implantation was similar to IVF. I had to give myself progesterone shots in the rear end for three weeks before my appointment. This prepared my body for pregnancy and increased the lining of my uterus, where the embryos hopefully would implant.

July 22, 2010 was set for our embryo transfer. The morning hours dragged on, and Daniel and I killed some time at Starbucks. I couldn't drink coffee and was so nervous I only sipped my tea. I kept myself together until we walked through the door of the doctor's office.

Babies Everywhere!

We're not going to have a baby. I couldn't keep the negative thoughts out of my head. Six years of sadness battled with the sprig of hope I'd allowed to grow inside me, and it all came out in a rush of tears.

The nurse moved me into an examination room, where I sobbed while Daniel talked with doctors in the hallway. I knew this would be an easy procedure, similar to an OB/GYN visit, but I couldn't get myself under control.

When the nurse told me that one of the three embryos had not survived the thawing out process, I cried even harder. Only after the nurse gave me medication to calm me down did I settle into the examination chair.

Daniel stood beside me as we watched the doctor transfer the two embryos that survived the thawing into my uterus. Thanks to a microscopic camera, we could see the entire process on a little screen. The ultrasound helped the doctor find the perfect place to implant each embryo. It gave us a window into the arrival of life.

The doctor was pleased with the procedure, but we had to wait two weeks to find out if it was successful.

I went back to the office for a blood test, and a nurse called soon after to reveal the results.

What if we're not pregnant? I thought as I put the call on speakerphone. *I don't know if I can handle more disappointment.*

Daniel and I both listened intently. We took in a collective breath and held it tight.

"The test was positive," she said, happily. "You're pregnant!"

Daniel and I locked eyes. *Did she just say what I think she said?*

The nurse had other news for us as well.

"There's a possibility it could be twins," she added.

We were in heaven.

Daniel and I collapsed to the floor, crying with joy. This truly was the happiest day of our lives. We called our parents, Maria and our best friends to tell them the news, and the happiness was so overwhelming that we did more crying together than talking.

After we shared the news with those closest to us, we decided to keep it a secret from everyone else until I was further along.

Along with this life-changing news, Daniel and I were moving to Boston where he had gotten a new job. When I interviewed for a job there, I felt obligated to share my news with one other person — my new boss.

"I'm seven weeks pregnant," I told her through a wide grin. "Nobody knows, not even my grandma." I smiled as the words I never thought I'd be able to say spilled out of my mouth.

The tests kept coming back positive, and my levels continued to indicate that I was probably carrying twins. But we knew the statistics on miscarriage, so we kept quiet and swore our parents to secrecy. When I hit the three-month mark, we spent several days calling friends and family across the country with our news. We revealed that

Babies Everywhere!

my pregnancy was through embryo adoption, and people were fascinated. My new OB/GYN, the nurses and our doctor friends had many questions about this new type of adoption.

I was as meticulous about my pregnancy as I had been about trying to get pregnant. I counted the twins' movements every day and enjoyed trying to figure out where each one was positioned.

Once an avid runner, I stopped during pregnancy to make sure I got enough rest. I ate exactly what the doctor told me to eat, and I slept as much as I was told to sleep. I was determined to make this the best pregnancy ever, but I still kept some of my joy at bay until we had crossed the 32-week mark — the age at which the twins could safely be born. Thankfully, I was still working, which kept me distracted. Otherwise, I might have monitored my pregnancy more compulsively.

༺༒༒༒༻

I flew back to Chicago when I was six months pregnant, to attend my own baby shower — finally. My mom, aunt and cousins hosted the event, and as I sat in the restaurant, surrounded by more than 75 friends and family members and a mountain of gifts for my unborn daughters, all I could do was thank God for this moment that I hardly could believe was happening.

I thanked God for the family who gave up their embryos so that we could have them. I thanked God for

Souls on Ice

the amazing people who loved us and had walked down the long, painful road of infertility with us. There was so much to celebrate.

At 36 weeks, the babies were so big that I felt like I could hardly breathe. I'm 5 feet, 3 inches, and I grew from 125 pounds to 215 during my pregnancy. I partly overcompensated for the doctor chiding me early on that I wasn't gaining enough weight. Because I was so closely monitored, doctors caught my preeclampsia early and sent me in for a C-section at 36 weeks and six days.

I was ready for the birth, but we were shocked when the doctor ordered me to go straight from a checkup to the hospital. We were having the babies that day! My mom had booked her plane ticket for the following week, and she hopped on an earlier flight that day. I wobbled into the hospital, so swollen from edema that I could hardly walk.

A twin delivery room is a high-risk situation, filled with doctors and nurses. Mine had additional residents and interns because it was a teaching hospital. Our daughters, Anna and Reagan, were born one minute apart amongst a crowd of people. Once resigned to possibly never having children, Daniel and I marveled at the extravagance of having two at once. For months afterward, I called Daniel several times a day to cry about how much I loved our family.

☙☙☙

Babies Everywhere!

While we were content with two babies, God wasn't finished blessing us.

When Anna and Reagan were 8 months old, Daniel and I took them with us on a trip to Chicago. We set up two cribs in a room at the Holiday Inn and settled in for the night, but I couldn't shake an uneasy feeling that something miraculous — completely unbelievable — was happening to my body.

"Daniel, I need you to run over to Walgreens and pick up two pregnancy tests."

Shocked, he obliged. Within an hour, we were huddled in the hotel room's tiny bathroom staring in shock at two clear pink lines on the test.

"Are you kidding me?" Daniel looked up with wide eyes.

We glanced out the bathroom door at our two sleeping babies.

Doctors said this could never happen. Ever.

I believe the miracle of me getting pregnant with the twins made it possible for me to get pregnant naturally with Kathy, who is 17 months younger than Anna and Reagan. Truly, we have babies everywhere!

◈◈◈

You'd think with three children under the age of 2 ½, we'd struggle. In reality, we've never been happier.

I've quit my job to stay home with the girls, and I revel in applying my organizational, planning and time-

Souls on Ice

management skills to my work as CEO of our house. I have a triple stroller, and I push the girls everywhere around town because one of the twins has severe carsickness. I love watching the twins crack each other up with their made-up language. Kathy, who we've nicknamed Godzilla, enjoys destroying every toy tower or castle the twins build. She loves her sisters and wants to do everything they do. Three kids in diapers may be a lot of work, but my biggest worry is when my girls turn 16!

We haven't let having three young children slow us down. A recent trip to Friendly's restaurant ended up with the typical chaos of three kids. Within 10 minutes we had a twin with a diaper explosion, food all over the floor and a baby climbing out of her high chair to crawl around on the ground.

Daniel and I caught each other's eyes and chuckled. After all that we've been through, how could we be upset? All we see, in the midst of what might look like a crazy mess in the middle of a restaurant, is the biggest blessing we could ever imagine.

"For with God NOTHING shall be impossible."
(Luke 1:37)

"Know that wisdom is such to your soul; if you find it, there will be a future, and your hope will not be cut off."
(Proverbs 24:14)

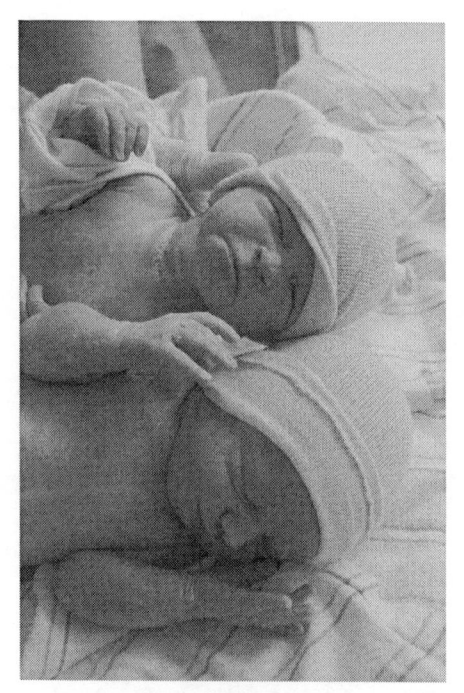

Babies Everywhere!

Twins Anna and Reagan

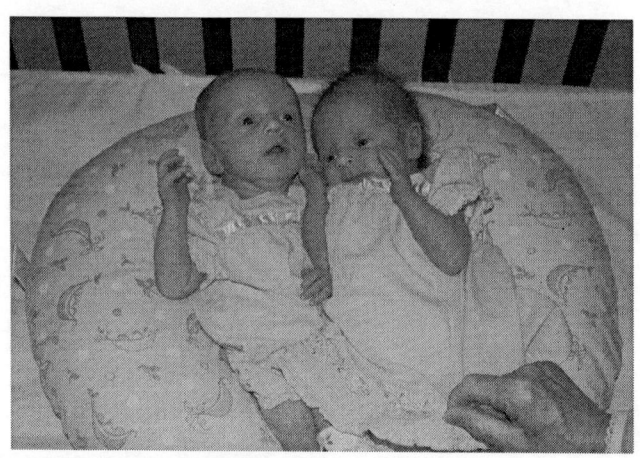

Twins Anna and Reagan

165

Surprise Blessings
The Adoption Story of Craig and Elena
Written by Karen Koczwara

Do we dare hope for you, little one?
Do we dare dream of you, sweet baby?
Do we dare wish that we'll hold you in
our arms one day?
You are wanted.
You are loved.
And so we wait.
We wait and wish and pray.
Until you are ours someday.

☙☙☙

It was the fall of 2008, and I was working in Seattle as a director of sales development for a systems integrator. I was traveling often. Seattle, with its hip, urban culture and outdoor activities, was the perfect place for a single guy like me. While I was happy with my routine, there was still a missing piece — a woman. I wanted someone to spend my life with, someone to endure the hardships and share in my joy as well. My friends convinced me to join eHarmony, a popular dating Web site.

When the site matched me with Elena's profile, I was immediately intrigued. Beautiful, with dark skin and long

Souls on Ice

dark hair, Elena also seemed to share many of my beliefs, values and interests. I contacted her and asked her out, but she canceled our first date. I remained persistent and asked her out again. She canceled a second time. But I did not give up. I asked her if I could call her after the holidays, and she said yes.

On January 4, 2009, Elena and I met for the first time. She asked me to pick her up and take her to get coffee. She walked out to my car wearing a pair of yoga pants, a puffy winter jacket and a scarf bundled around her head. She wasn't wearing makeup because she didn't want my opinion of her to be based on her looks. Even so, I couldn't help but notice her smile and her bright, beautiful eyes.

"I have a yoga class to go to, so I've only got about 45 minutes," she explained sweetly.

I was happy to have just a few minutes of her time. We chatted over our coffee and seemed to hit it off. Elena told me she'd moved from Maui to Seattle in July to pursue her doctorate. I was impressed by her intelligence, but also by her faith in God. I asked her out again, and we began dating. As we got to know one another, Elena opened up to me. She explained her initial hesitancy to meet me, confiding that she'd gone through a difficult heartbreak in a prior relationship.

We visited my church, where the pastor came up to speak with me, as well as several of my friends. Elena was impressed that I seemed so well connected, as it was very important to her to find a man with a strong faith in God.

Surprise Blessings

After a month of dating, she asked me pointedly, "What are your intentions?" Elena worked for the University of Hawaii and had not intended to stay permanently in Seattle. I could tell she was starting to consider me as a potential partner for life.

I expressed to her that I took our relationship seriously. I was all in. She agreed, and I knew that we were on the same page. About three months into our relationship, I knew she was it for me. We fell hard for each other. We got engaged in July, and on November 21, we married. We wed in Seattle and then went back to Maui in December for a reception with all of Elena's family and friends. We were excited to start our new life together.

As "me" turned to "we," Elena and I began thinking about "us." To our surprise and delight, Elena got pregnant that October 2010, just a month after we started trying. Because we were not as young as some couples, we hadn't expected things to happen so quickly. We grew excited about being able to tell friends and family that we were expecting.

Though it was too early to hear the baby's heartbeat, Elena and I already loved the tiny little baby inside her tummy. We both believed that life began at the moment of conception, and we knew God already had a plan for that child. But his plan would prove to be much different than ours.

At 4 a.m. one morning, Elena awoke and began to bleed. Unsure of what was happening, we called our friend

Souls on Ice

who was a nurse. She advised us to go to the hospital. By 7 a.m. we found ourselves in a tiny room where doctors told us she had lost the baby. The grief was awful. We realized that we'd never get to hold the child we'd already come to love.

"When I was bleeding, I said, 'God, I pray this isn't your will, but if it is, take our love with him or her,'" Elena told me through her tears. "I know we will see our baby in heaven someday, but this is still so hard."

I felt my wife's sadness along with my own. We'd already felt like the parents of that child. We had wanted that little one and had dreams for him or her. Now there was an emptiness in place of those dreams. We continued to grieve, mourning our loss but also trusting that God cared about us. We began trying again for a child, but Elena did not conceive. The following spring, we decided to investigate any potential medical problems to see why we were having difficulty getting pregnant on our own.

We visited our first fertility clinic in March 2011, to explore our options. Our experience was not what we had hoped for. Fertility methods, we learned, could be expensive and harrowing. "You've got to do in vitro fertilization," the doctor said flatly. "You're not having a baby on your own." Sad and discouraged, we began to explore other options.

In June, we began to discuss adoption. We researched different adoption processes, including foster, international and domestic adoption. While we knew this could be a wonderful option, it also came with its own set of challenges. I wasn't convinced this was the right path for us.

The doctor at the first fertility clinic had a bedside manner that was lacking, and we weren't sure IVF was the only option, so we decided to try a different clinic. In late June, we visited a reproductive clinic where the doctors suggested that we try IUI, or intrauterine insemination. We discussed it and decided to give it a try. We underwent three rounds of the procedure, but each time, it failed. The doctors increased Elena's medication, but her body still did not respond the way we'd hoped. After the third try, we grew more disheartened than ever.

We revisited the idea of adoption. Though we'd dreamed of having our own biological children, we also wanted to be open to what God had for us. We knew families came about in all sorts of ways, and adoption could be a beautiful thing.

We met with a woman named Lavonne from our home church. Lavonne and her husband had adopted four special needs children from China, and they had a wealth of information to share. They explained the process they'd gone through, the challenges they'd faced and the rewards that had come from watching these beautiful children grow. Though Elena was excited after the meeting, I had some initial reservations.

"Wow, I had no idea how hard the process of adoption could be," I told her, my head spinning.

But we continued to pray, asking God to show us how he wanted us to proceed. In the meantime, we planned a trip back to Maui in December to visit Elena's family for Christmas. Before we left for Maui, we ran into Lavonne again at church, and she made an interesting proposal.

"I recently spoke with Maria Lancaster, who heads up the Embryo Adoption Program at Cedar Park Church. She told me that she has a Japanese embryo and asked me if I knew of a family that would be a potential match." Lavonne knew that I was Japanese and Elena was Spanish and Portuguese. "I immediately thought of you and Elena."

On New Year's Eve, as fireworks lit up the night sky, Elena and I prayed and wished for a baby. "Maybe. Just maybe, we'll have a baby next year."

In January 2012, we decided to follow up with the fertility clinic to find out the next step. The doctor delivered some discouraging words. "You have less than a 1 percent chance of conceiving naturally," he told us. "With an IUI, you have a 5 to 15 percent chance of conceiving. And with in vitro fertilization, you have less than a 35 percent chance of having a child."

One percent chance of conceiving naturally. My heart sank, as did Elena's. This was not the news we had hoped for.

"I thought the IUI would work," Elena told the doctor, defeated. "Why did you suggest this to us?"

"Everyone responds differently," the doctor replied apologetically. "There's always the IVF route. Would you like to consider that?"

Elena and I prayed about IVF. We knew it could get

Surprise Blessings

quite expensive, and we didn't have the $30,000 it would cost for such a procedure. We'd already experienced the pain of a miscarriage, followed by months of trying to conceive. Enduring more loss seemed unbearable. Were we willing to go down another potentially long and painful road?

We continued to seek God through our sadness, trying to understand his purpose in all of it. Elena and I both came from large families and had always dreamed of having little ones. We'd imagined picnics, birthday parties and cozy holidays spent eating and laughing together. We wanted a child to raise, love, nurture and teach about God's love. We loved each other and had the means to provide a nice home for a baby. We'd never imagined it would be so difficult to conceive. What did God have in mind for us?

Elena and I were still broken over the failed IUIs. "God has placed the desire in our hearts to have children," I told Elena. "He knows how badly we want a child. We will continue to trust in him." But with each passing week, it became more difficult. We began to wonder if we'd ever have a child of our own. Was this not God's plan for us? Family gatherings were becoming increasingly difficult, full of smiling babies that weren't our own. And I knew that Elena was drowning in anger and sadness.

In January, Elena contacted Maria.

"Families who have undergone in vitro fertilization and have frozen their embryos can choose to adopt them out to another family," Maria explained. "Those embryos are then implanted into the uterus of the adoptive mother, and she can enjoy the pregnancy and birth of a baby just as if it were her own biological child. It's really a win/win situation. Those families adopting out the embryos are reassured that these precious lives are preserved, and those who adopt them get the chance to bring a child into the world."

"Wow, that's really cool!" Elena gushed. "I had no idea something like that existed."

Maria encouraged us to check out Cedar Park Church to learn more about the program. On January 21, we visited the church and watched an impactful movie, *The Gift of Life*. Hosted by former Arkansas Governor Mike Huckabee, the movie explored the issue of the sanctity of life and featured several individuals whose mothers had seriously considered aborting them. It served as a great reminder that life begins at conception and that all life is valuable, no matter the circumstances.

After the movie, Maria spoke about Presentation Sunday, which was to take place at the church the following week. The service was a special time set aside each year to pray specifically for those struggling with infertility. Parents who had undergone embryo adoption would be there with their children to share their stories. Elena and I looked forward to the service, eager to meet these families who had already gone through this journey.

"I'm not totally sure about this," I told my wife. "But I'm open to learning more about it. This just might be what we've been looking for."

Surprise Blessings

The following Sunday, we arrived again at Cedar Park Church. The families with children born through embryo adoption stepped up to share their remarkable stories, and the congregation prayed over them. The pastor then opened up the service to anyone else who wanted prayer. Elena and I went forward, along with roughly 70 other people.

As we glanced around, my heart went out to them. These were other people just like us, people who had prayed and hoped and waited for a baby. Their hearts, too, were breaking. We had felt isolated thus far on our journey, but as I saw them kneeling at the altar there beside us, I realized we were not alone.

I bowed my head and closed my eyes, and as people began to pray over us, I felt God speak to my heart.

Did you come to Cedar Park because you are embarrassed to be prayed for at your own church?

No.

Now that you have humbled yourself, I will bless you.

When, God?

Craig, I will bless you. Your child will glorify me.

I wept tears of joy as one woman began praying over us. "Thank you, Jesus," she murmured over and over. And then another woman spoke the powerful words I will never, ever forget.

"God will bless you with a child. You will be back next year with a child," she said directly to me.

Thank you, God! Oh, thank you!

After the service, I told Elena how God had touched

my heart. "He is going to bless us with a baby," I assured her.

"Really?" Elena's eyes filled with tears.

I saw the pain in her eyes, and I knew how she felt. Did we dare keep hoping and dreaming? Ironically, Elena had been getting her doctorate in health and wellness. At one time, she had struggled with an eating disorder, and her experience had led her to pursue that particular career path. No matter how much she studied up on our current situation, however, she could not control it. We were both learning that God was fully in control, and we had to completely surrender the situation to him. As the Bible reads, he knew the number of hairs on our heads and had known us even before we were born. We had to trust that he knew the child we were to have and just how that child was to come into the world.

"I'm really excited about embryo adoption," I told Elena. "I think this might be an answer to our prayers. I'm ready to move forward."

"Me, too," Elena agreed. "I'm ready to do this."

We began the process of embryo adoption, filling out the necessary papers to apply. Much like a traditional adoption, the process required background checks, medical checks, a home study and other personal information. We completed it all and sent it off, then waited and prayed. I thought again of the woman's words at the prayer service: "You will have a child." I wondered if she was right. Would one of those embryos turn into a little baby we'd someday soon hold in our arms?

Surprise Blessings

We made a book for our potential embryo donor family, including photos of our families, our hobbies and our environment. Donor families would have a chance to flip through it and choose us if they felt we were the right fit.

I grew more excited at the prospect of partnering with another family to bring a child into the world. God had opened a door for us in an unexpected way, and we could not wait to see what he did.

In March, we took a vacation to Mexico to take our mind off of things. While there, we learned there'd been a glitch with some of Elena's paperwork she'd had to obtain from Hawaii. Because of logistics, we'd be forced to push back the application process by a month. We were discouraged by the news, as we'd hoped to move forward as quickly as possible.

"So many hoops to jump through! Why can nothing be easy?" Elena cried, frustrated. "Why is it that people everywhere get pregnant all the time, yet I can't have a baby?" Tears were rolling down her cheeks.

Again, I felt my wife's pain. As much as we tried to trust in God for his perfect plan, it was still difficult to understand why he'd not allowed us to have a child of our own thus far. We were loving, stable and eager to raise a child. We held to good values and planned to raise our child in the ways of God. If children were supposed to be a blessing, why had we not been blessed? Infertility sometimes felt like a harsh slap to the face. It just didn't seem fair. But God had given me a word in the prayer meeting that day, and I strongly believed he would fulfill it. We were not sure how the story would play out, but I chose to believe he would give us the greatest desire of our heart.

The following weekend, we attended a family event for Easter. We knew there would be children there, and we prayed it would not be too difficult. *God, let this be a joyful time, not a painful time.*

It wasn't long before we received some wonderful news. A donor family had selected us to adopt their embryo! A Japanese family, they truly wanted another Japanese couple to have their child. Though we did not meet in person, they sent photos of their children, and we exchanged e-mails back and forth.

"I feel like God led you to us," the mother told us.

Our excitement mounted. We now had a donor and could officially move forward. We were going to have a baby!

In April, we met with a social worker for a final evaluation prior to transferring the embryo. We learned that once Elena had her next period, we needed to schedule the transfer accordingly. On April 9, we were notified that our embryo had been shipped to Seattle. That night, on our way home from our small group Bible study, Elena informed me that she wanted to take a pregnancy test.

"I know the fertility doctor said that we have less than a 1 percent chance of conceiving without medical intervention," she said, "but I still haven't had my period,

Surprise Blessings

and I'm anxious to take the final test and schedule the transfer after the paperwork holdup."

When we arrived home, Elena took the home pregnancy test, and we waited. When two little pink lines showed up on the stick, Elena stared at it in disbelief.

I stared at the stick with her, unable to believe my eyes. Sure enough, two pink lines winked back at us. *A baby! We are going to have a baby!* It was a true miracle. "I'm pregnant!" she said. "I'm really pregnant! How can this be?!" Soon, we were both crying tears of shock and joy.

We sank into the couch and turned on worship music, soaking up the beautiful moment and praising God. "I can't believe it," I muttered. "This is the best news in the world."

"Do you realize that if we hadn't had to jump through all those hoops, the doctors would have put me on birth control by this time, and we would not be sitting here right now?" Elena whispered in awe. "I just can't believe it."

The next day, however, our elation turned to anxiety. What if something went wrong with the pregnancy again? We'd already lost one child to miscarriage. What if it happened again? We decided to hold off on telling friends and family and kept the news to ourselves for a while. We scheduled an appointment with our family doctor to be absolutely sure the results were positive. Three tests later, we knew it was true. Elena was really carrying our baby!

Six weeks later, I went in with her for an ultrasound. As Elena lay on the bed in the doctor's office, a tiny little heartbeat appeared on the screen before us. A real live little heartbeat. A baby inside of her, already growing. We could scarcely believe our eyes.

The nurse smiled at our happy news. "This is truly amazing. I am so happy for you guys."

"Can you believe it happened naturally?" Elena smiled back.

My mind drifted to the doctor's words almost a year before. *You have a 1 percent chance of conceiving on your own.* After experiencing a devastating miscarriage, undergoing fertility treatment, exploring traditional adoption and then going through the process of embryo adoption, we'd never imagined in a million years that we'd be sitting in a doctor's office experiencing such joy. *God, you surely are amazing. You have answered our prayers in a most unexpected way, and we are so grateful. This is your baby. We trust you with his or her life.*

We began routine exams with an obstetrician and had the chance to listen to the heartbeat as it got stronger and stronger. Elena continued to grapple with fear, and I understood her concerns. Every mother who has experienced loss struggles to hope and dream again. We prayed over the baby constantly, trusting that God would see this pregnancy to the very end.

"When does the worrying stop?" Elena asked the doctor one day.

The doctor laughed. "Oh, just wait till the baby is born. Then a whole new set of worries begin."

We hadn't even thought of that. We'd been so

Surprise Blessings

concerned about just bringing the baby safely into the world, we'd forgotten about all that came afterward. What if the child got hurt or sick? What if we didn't know how to be good parents? Again, we took our concerns to God. We'd worry about that stuff later.

Elena experienced heavy morning sickness throughout her pregnancy, but she did not complain once. "It is such a privilege to be pregnant," she told me, her face glowing. "I'll gladly take this any day." Though we had not found out the sex of the baby, Elena was sure it was a little girl.

As Elena's belly grew, I began to get more excited. *This is real! This is happening!* When the baby jumped beneath her skin, I practically jumped as well. *That's our baby in there! A little life, getting stronger and bigger every day!*

Elena's prediction was correct. We learned we were having a little girl. We discussed names and landed on Kalea Grace. Kalea means "joy" in Hawaiian, and Grace seemed especially fitting, as it means "undeserved gift." We felt that was exactly what we'd been given — an undeserved gift. We had done nothing to earn it, but God, in his wonderful love, had bestowed it upon us.

As Elena's due date approached, our doctor asked us what sort of birth plan we wanted.

"The kind where you bring the baby home," Elena replied with a smile.

On December 14, little Kalea Grace entered the world at 1:42 a.m. As we held her in our arms, we rejoiced, thanking God for such a beautiful miracle. With 10 tiny fingers and 10 tiny toes, she was absolutely perfect.

Souls on Ice

Immediately, all the fear Elena had struggled with dissipated when she held her little girl. As we sat there together, relishing the moment, we realized we had at last become "us."

Our family and friends were overjoyed. They knew we had walked a long, hard road, and they could not wait to congratulate us. With Christmas just around the corner, we had much to celebrate — Jesus' birth and the birth of our precious daughter.

On January 27, 2013, we gave our testimony on Presentation Sunday at Cedar Park Church. It was an honor to return to the place where our journey had begun. I again remembered the woman who had prayed over me exactly a year before, confirming that God would give us a child one year later. That day, we stood before a congregation to announce that God had answered our prayers in a mighty way.

Our pastor at our home church, Westminster Chapel, asked us to share our story, too. After opening up about our experience, many people in our lives came up to share that they'd struggled with infertility as well. Like ours, some of their journeys were extremely painful, but many of them never got angry with God. Instead, they trusted him for his perfect plan, and in the end, God blessed them. We knew that not all stories ended with a baby, but God's plan was more fulfilling than anything anyone could have asked for.

Though we were thrilled about Kalea's birth, we did not forget the embryo we had adopted. We strongly

Surprise Blessings

believed that the embryo, like little Kalea, was a gift from God, and we did not take that gift lightly. I often thought about the donor family's children as the image of their little faces popped into my head. Though we'd never met them, we had a special connection with this family. We continued to store the embryo, and in the meantime, we prayed for it as though it was already our child. *God, we know you have a plan for this embryo. We believe you brought us on this journey for a reason, and we believe that life of every kind is a gift. We will wait on you for what's next.*

సాసాసా

"Quick! Look! She's doing it again!" Elena called out.

I glanced over and laughed, watching little Kalea doing the army crawl across the floor with her sweet, pudgy little arms. Now 9 months old, she met all the milestones perfectly — eating solid foods, making all sorts of noises and now moving herself around. It was hard to believe that in just a few months, we'd celebrate her first birthday. The year had certainly flown.

I still worked in sales, and Elena now taught pre- and post-natal yoga classes at studios and athletic clubs. We soaked up every precious moment with our good-natured little baby, knowing how quickly she would grow. In our spare time, we enjoyed walking down the bustling Seattle streets, serving in ministry, spending time with friends and family and attending sporting events. Most of all, we enjoyed meeting with other parents and their little ones. We loved sharing our story, starting with our infertility journey and ending with the miracle of Kalea. It was a story we would never tire of sharing, because each time we did, God got all the glory.

Elena shared with me that she'd grown so much in her faith in God through our experience. She'd learned to trust in him, she'd learned that he was in complete control and she'd learned that each child, no matter how they came into the world or into a family, was a true miracle and gift from God. Kalea's middle name, Grace, reminded us of this undeserved gift every day.

We continued to pray for our precious frozen embryo and decided that in January 2014, we'd go through with the transfer. Perhaps a brother or sister would soon join little Kalea, rounding out our family to four. I grew excited, imaging that little embryo transforming into a baby inside Elena's belly. God had done one miracle, and we believed he could and would do another. What a privilege and a gift to give another little life a chance.

When I first saw Elena bundled up in the borrowed puffy jacket, I'd never imagined our journey would lead where it had. It's been painful, even harrowing at times. There have been many tears. Enduring the miscarriage was especially hard. But in the end, we would not take anything back, because in the process, God taught us so much about himself. We've learned that his timing is perfect, that he is always in control and that he can bring good through heartache. He loves us deeply, just as we

Surprise Blessings

loved the children we'd never even met. Our experiences rocked our faith and our relationships with God. Because of our faith and in spite of our anger, Jesus blessed us beyond measure. Our story is *to be continued*, and we cannot wait to see it unfold.

> "Not only that, but we rejoice in our sufferings, knowing that suffering produces endurance, and endurance produces character, and character produces hope, and hope does not put us to shame, because God's love has been poured into our hearts through the Holy Spirit who has been given to us." (Romans 5:3-5 ESV)

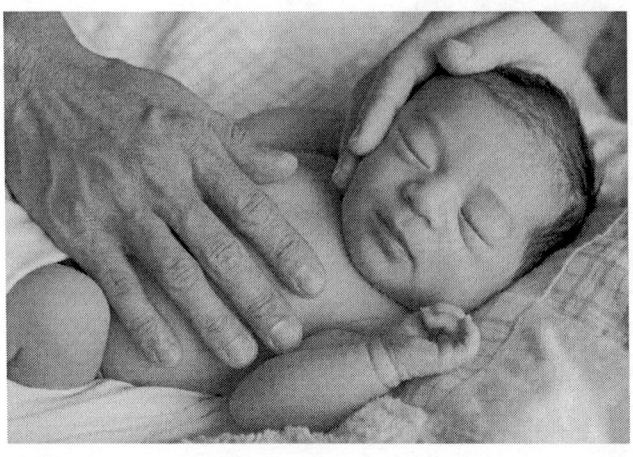

Kalea Grace

Souls on Ice

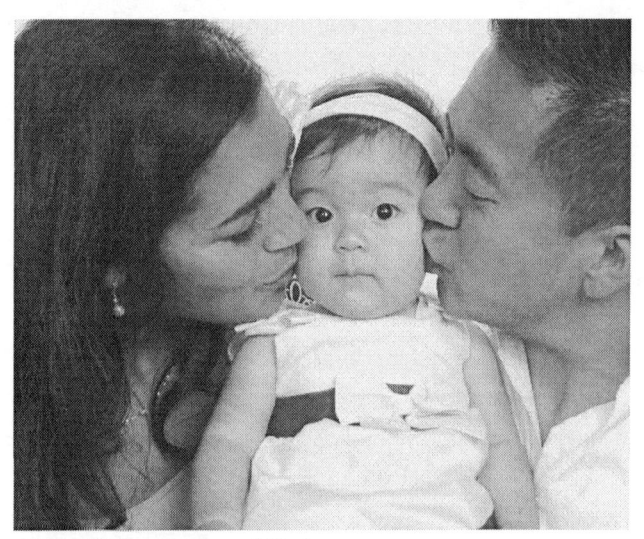

Elena, Kalea Grace and Craig

Craig, Elena and Kalea Grace

The Giving
The Donating Story of Lisa and Mark
Written by Karen Koczwara

Mark and I were both graduate students at Michigan State University and the University of Illinois when friends first introduced us. I was working on my doctorate, and Mark had just completed the requirements for his doctorate and was teaching in Indiana. We married in 1990 in Washington State, where we planned to pursue our respective careers in economics and instructional development and technology.

Both career-minded professionals, we were accustomed to having things go as planned. We looked forward to starting a family, never imagining that we would have trouble conceiving. But when we did not get pregnant right away, we realized that we might have to set aside our well-laid plans. And thus began a journey we never imagined we'd embark on, one that would take us through heartache, joy and everything in between.

As the months and years passed and we still did not conceive, we decided to consult with fertility doctors. We visited five different fertility clinics, trying to gain an understanding of our challenges and options. The information we gained varied, and we did our best to try to sort through it all. After undergoing several tests, we

Souls on Ice

learned that the only way we'd ever be able to have a child of our own would be through in vitro fertilization. We very much wanted a child and were willing to do whatever it took to have one. But we also knew God was ultimately in control of our situation, and so we trusted in him for his perfect timing.

Mark and I continued to focus on our careers and also got involved in ministry. We felt God leading us to be a part of an international mission organization. All the while, we continued to wait and pray, wait and pray and wait and pray some more.

In vitro fertilization, as many know, is not an easy process. It can be an emotional rollercoaster, filled with ups and downs, hormonal surprises, unexpected twists and turns and many painful detours. Mark and I turned to God each step of the way, relying on our faith in him. We shed many tears, wondering if we'd ever bring home our own little bundle of joy. We chose the path of in vitro, knowing it was our strongest chance of getting pregnant. We then waited for the pregnancy test to reveal good news.

In mid-2003, 13 years after we were married, we received the long-awaited good news. We were going to have a baby at last! God had answered our fervent prayers.

We proceeded cautiously, not wanting to get too excited after a series of heartbreaking letdowns. We decided to keep a low profile with the pregnancy and wait as long as possible before telling all our friends and family. My doctor encouraged me that the pregnancy was going

The Giving

along smoothly and even suggested I try swimming. I had always been active and looked forward to continuing my exercise routine. As my seventh month approached and my belly swelled with life, I finally felt that I could breathe a sigh of relief. *Thank you, God,* I prayed. *I am trusting that you will bring this pregnancy full term and this baby safely into the world.*

The doctor scheduled a C-section for me around my due date in January 2004. Mark traveled overseas in his work as a project funding coordinator. He returned a few days before the scheduled C-section, and we packed our hospital bags, eagerly anticipating the big day. At last, it arrived.

Things went as smoothly as possible, and little Joshua made his grand debut, weighing a healthy 6 1/2 pounds. Mark was in the delivery room and cut the umbilical cord. As we held our miracle baby in our arms for the first time, we rejoiced, shedding tears of joy as we thanked God for this wonderful gift of life. Little did we know that nearly 10 years later, another couple we'd never met would welcome their own miracle baby into the world, and we would play a special part in their story.

Our friends and family were elated when they learned about Joshua's birth. Many of them were shocked because we'd been so quiet about our journey. Congratulatory cards and letters showed up in the mailbox, and we cherished every one of them. At one point, we'd wondered if we'd ever have a child of our own. Now, thanks to God's goodness, we had reason to celebrate.

Souls on Ice

Our ministry required us to relocate to Europe, and we lived there until 2007, awaiting a new mission assignment. Meanwhile, life marched on, and Joshua grew from a robust baby to an active toddler and then a thriving little boy. As he got older, we loved watching him do all the typical things boys enjoy — running, biking, fishing, kicking the soccer ball and playing computer games. He enjoyed school and brought home straight A's. We could not have been more proud of him. When we looked at Joshua, we saw not just a healthy, active, brown-eyed little boy, but a living, breathing miracle. He was our gift from heaven.

We paid to store the remaining frozen embryos from our in vitro fertilization process. Our doctor assured us we could store them indefinitely. While we'd heard other doctors recommend that their patients donate their remaining embryos to science, our doctor never suggested it. He had a strong faith in God and believed that life begins at conception. Discarding these embryos, in his opinion, would be discarding life. Though we agreed, we did not know what the future held for them. But that was all about to change.

While visiting our church in Seattle one Sunday, we learned about a woman named Maria, who'd started a unique embryo adoption program. The speaker explained that through embryo adoption, couples who were not able to conceive on their own could adopt frozen embryos from other couples who had already undergone the in vitro process. The adopting couple would be able to go

The Giving

through with a pregnancy just as if they'd conceived on their own, and in the end, that once-frozen embryo would result in a beautiful baby.

As Mark and I heard the message, our hearts began to stir. We had never given embryo adoption any thought before, but suddenly, the idea made so much sense. We, too, believed life began at conception and that each of those frozen embryos was a potential life. The program seemed like a win/win. We'd have a chance to donate our frozen embryos, and another couple struggling to conceive would be given hope.

"This is so exciting," I told Mark. "I think this is what we are meant to do! It means a lot to me to think that no human life will be destroyed in this process."

We looked into the program, and we decided to register our embryos. The program director explained that choosing our adoptive family could be an elaborate process. She encouraged us to take our time to select just the right couple for our embryos.

Jason and Kate were the second couple introduced to us. They sent a beautiful book filled with photos of their home, their wedding day, their friends and family and their hobbies. They described themselves and reiterated their desire to have a child of their own. While we were impressed with them overall, one thing especially stood out to us — their love for God. It was very important for us to find a couple who shared our faith and would raise their child in a home similar to ours. Mark and I discussed them, prayed and then called the program director, Maria.

Souls on Ice

"We've made our choice," we told her with confidence. "We choose Jason and Kate."

To our delight, Jason and Kate were happy to be matched with us. Our embryos could be easily transferred from the storage facility straight to Jason and Kate. The young couple adopted five embryos, willing to have five children if all five became viable. In the meantime, we prayed, asking God to bless them on their journey. And with each passing day, we grew more excited. We had been in their shoes and knew the heartache of infertility all too well. We, too, had hardly dared to dream, not sure if we'd ever assemble a crib, change a diaper or plant kisses on our own baby's soft, chubby cheeks. Joshua was our little miracle, a thriving reminder of God's faithfulness in our lives. Now it was Jason and Kate's turn.

We asked God to give them a miracle, too.

> "For you formed my inward parts; you covered me in my mother's womb. I will praise you, for I am fearfully and wonderfully made; marvelous are your works, and *that* my soul knows very well. My frame was not hidden from you, when I was made in secret, and skillfully wrought in the lowest parts of the earth. Your eyes saw my substance, being yet unformed, and in your book they all were written, the days fashioned for me, when *as yet there were* none of them." (Psalm 139:13-16)

The Heart of a Miracle
The Adoption Story of Jason and Kate McKenzie
Written by Karen Koczwara

Dear Sweet Pea,

Baby, my heart is sad tonight. Because my whole life I've dreamed of you. Our whole marriage we've talked about you. We want to be able to bring you into this world, to raise you, to love you, to share you with everyone. And now, well, we just don't know if that's ever going to happen.

In our heart of hearts we both feel like we were made to love you. I want to be your mom with every ounce of my being. And your father, well, he would be an amazing father. He wants you to be introduced to this world just as much as I do.

Ironically, we love you, and we want you, and we don't even know if you're ever going to exist.

We wait. We pray. We hope.

Because, baby, I can promise you this. If God allows us the blessing of you, we will commit ourselves to loving you, providing for you, teaching you, walking alongside you, praying for you and protecting you … all the days of our lives.

So until then,
Mommy and Daddy

Souls on Ice

❧❧❧

Jason and I met at a small Christian college in Pennsylvania. He was from Washington State, and I was from New York. We first crossed paths our freshman year, began dating our junior year and were engaged by our senior year. We eagerly began planning our wedding, counting the days until our lives meshed into one. Like most young couples, we looked forward to starting a family. Jason was one of six siblings, and though I was an only child, I'd always dreamed of having several little ones running around my feet. We chose to settle in the area of Washington where Jason had grown up. We planned to travel a bit, then settle down and start trying for a family. If things went as planned, we'd soon be toting a little pink or blue bundle of joy, happily pushing a stroller down a street lined with picket fences.

But things did not go as planned.

Jason and I were both young and healthy and had no reason to believe we would not conceive right away. In early December 2007, while washing dishes, I felt God speak to my heart, asking me to invite him into the conversation about starting a family. I'd been so caught up in daydreaming about having a child of our own that I hadn't stopped to actually talk with God about it. In that moment, I stopped what I was doing and prayed, giving the entire situation up to him. As I washed the last of the suds down the drain, I smiled through my tears. *Surely,*

The Heart of a Miracle

this must be God's blessing, his way of giving me permission to start trying to get pregnant. It's time!

We did not get pregnant right away, but we remained hopeful. However, as the months passed, we grew a bit concerned. After two and a half years, I went to the doctor to get checked out. When my tests came back normal, we breathed a sigh of relief. Jason then underwent a series of tests, and on June 4, 2010, the doctors delivered some discouraging news. He had zero motility, which meant we would not be able to conceive naturally.

That explains it! We were relieved to have some answers. "This is not your fault," I tried to encourage him, doing my best to stay composed. Little did we know our situation wasn't quite that simple.

Though our doctor decided to focus on Jason's infertility issues, he scheduled me for a routine exam the following month. During the visit, he performed a hysterosalpingogram by inserting dye into my uterus. "We're checking to see if the dye flows through both of your fallopian tubes and into your abdominal cavity," he explained.

To my shock, the doctor discovered that not one but both of my tubes were completely blocked. I stared at him, incredulous, as the news sank in.

"There is a surgical procedure I recommend," the doctor said, but my mind was already racing. *How can this be? You're telling me that both my husband and I have fertility issues? That we might never have children of our own?*

Souls on Ice

Devastation overwhelmed me as I walked to my car in a daze. I had just started a new job and wondered how I'd be able to function. *This can't be happening,* I repeated to myself. I called Jason and shared the news with him at my work.

Jason did his best to encourage me. "We'll get the surgery. Change our diets. Do whatever we have to do," he said emphatically. "This isn't the end for us, Kate."

But I wasn't so sure. Inside, I was crumbling. I had dreamed of having children since I was a little girl. The idea of not being able to conceive was beyond devastating. As my emotions took over, I shifted my blame to God. *Why did you allow this to happen?* I railed at him. *This isn't fair!*

The next day, I wrote a letter to our baby, addressing a child I wasn't sure we'd ever have. Brokenhearted, I poured my words onto paper. As tears spilled down my cheeks, I explained to the child that if we ever had the chance to hold him or her in our arms, we'd be the very best parents we could possibly be. I'd lain awake so many nights, picturing a little girl with dark hair like mine or a little boy with bright blue eyes like Jason's. I'd envisioned decorating a nursery, picking out little clothes, shopping for diapers and watching my belly swell with life. I'd never imagined we'd be dealt such a painful blow as this.

We spent the next few weeks grieving and weighing our options. In vitro fertilization was a possibility, though we knew it would be quite costly. Adoption was another thought. We didn't know any close friends who'd adopted,

The Heart of a Miracle

and we initially resented the idea of not having our own biological children. A third option was to love the children already in our lives and look for other youngsters to mentor. This still did not fulfill our heart's desire to have a child of our own. And then there was a fourth option — a miracle of God. We'd heard amazing stories and knew anything was possible with him. Which one of these roads would we walk down?

I raced home from work each day and opened my Bible, searching for some hope. I read the story of a woman named Hannah, who'd been told she'd never have a child. But God had given her a little boy named Samuel — her very own miracle baby. Would God do the same for me?

Some days I focused on hope as I tried to trust in God. Other days I grew angry and had to ask God to save me from becoming bitter. I knew bitterness only led to despair, and I tried not to focus on that. Instead, I turned my eyes back up to God and prayed. *This is your story, God. I don't know what you're doing, but you write it. Give me grace in the midst of this heartache.*

Meanwhile, Jason struggled with his own grief process. While he'd initially remained optimistic, he grew disheartened as the reality set in. Not only was he one of six siblings, but his parents were both one of six as well. His uncle had often joked that the male side of his family was especially "potent." He'd dreamed along with me about having at least two or three kids, dressing them in cute clothes and taking the requisite Christmas photos

Souls on Ice

together. Slowly, the realization that that dream would not come true sank in, and he was faced with the same questions I wrestled with.

Jason and I continued to explore international, domestic and foster adoption, all the while leaning toward finding a way to have a child of our own. I began meeting with people, sharing our story with them as we discussed our options. One day, I stumbled upon a Christian blog that caught my eye. A woman shared how she had undergone the process of embryo adoption and was now pregnant. My heart leapt as I read her story, a sliver of hope creeping in. Was this an option for us?

I did extensive research and learned as much as I could about embryo adoption. I learned that when couples choose to do in vitro fertilization, they have multiple eggs that are harvested and fertilized. These fertilized eggs create embryos, which they later have implanted with the purpose of getting pregnant. The rest of the embryos are frozen and stored for future use. But if the parents no longer want or need the embryos, they are given the option to donate them to science or discard them. The third option, which few people knew about, was the miracle of embryo adoption.

During embryo adoption, the embryos are transferred and implanted into another woman's uterus, and that woman gets to experience a normal pregnancy just as if she'd naturally conceived herself.

The donor parents sign legal documents, turning over all rights and responsibilities for the child to the adoptive

The Heart of a Miracle

parents. As I continued to read through the facts, my eyes darted to a startling statistic. *In 2003, there were 400,000 frozen embryos in America. They were sitting on shelves. Only about 9,000 will actually be adopted.*

Four hundred thousand. I gulped hard. Because I believed that life began at conception, I knew that each of these frozen embryos was a potential life. A little boy or girl, just waiting for a mom and dad to give them a chance. What if one of those frozen embryos was our future child?

I had never heard of embryo adoption before, but suddenly, it was all I could think about. I broached the subject with Jason, and to my surprise, he was beyond excited. Neither of us had felt complete peace about traditional adoption or in vitro fertilization. But as we discussed this new option, it seemed to make perfect sense. We continued to pray and do research, and with each passing day, we grew more and more eager to start the process.

"I really think this is what we're supposed to do. And I don't want to wait. I want it to happen now," I told Jason. My kind husband whisked me off to Babies R Us to look at cribs, my eyes dancing as we mulled over the different designs.

I stared at the cribs, daring to dream for just a moment. Would we ever buy one? Could I picture a tiny baby sleeping peacefully in one of them? We trusted God to guide us in our decision, while practically jumping out of our skin with excitement. *I know this must be you, God, preparing us for this adventure,* I prayed.

Souls on Ice

I called my doctor's office and learned that they were able to do embryo transfers. They referred me to a few different agencies, most of which were in Tennessee and California. I'd heard of all but one of them — an agency an hour and a half from our house in Washington!

I left work at 5 p.m. and called the agency, not expecting anyone to answer. To my surprise, a woman picked up the phone. She introduced herself as Maria Lancaster, the director of the program, and we talked for 15 minutes.

"My husband and I were one of the first couples in the United States to undergo embryo adoption six years ago," she explained. "I have a real passion for this process and started a ministry through our church last year to bring more awareness to it. This Sunday, actually, our church is celebrating the first birth through this program. We'd love for you and your husband to come to the service and the lunch afterward. Several other embryo adoption couples will be there for you to meet."

"This Sunday?" I repeated.

This is too good to be true — a total answer to our prayers!

"Yes." Maria's voice was sweet and supportive. "This is your divine appointment," she added.

A divine appointment. I hung up the phone, practically dancing with joy. *This Sunday! We could be ready to embark on the biggest adventure of our lives!*

I e-mailed my doctor to see if, based on my infertility diagnosis, he thought I would be a good candidate for

The Heart of a Miracle

embryo adoption. He wrote back within a few hours with some good news.

Dear Kate: You are absolutely a candidate for a healthy embryo transfer. I am happy to help in any way with respect to embryo adoption.

A certain peace overwhelmed me as I read his words. *Somewhere out there is a baby that is meant to be ours. God is in the center of this. We are going to trust in him and see where this path leads, even if it's not all roses and butterflies along the way. We are ready to do this!*

On Sunday, September 19, we made the drive to Cedar Park Church in Bothell. We walked through the doors, still not sure what to expect, and discovered the band had just started the first worship song.

The church dedicated the entire service to embryo adoption. They brought in a highly renowned scientist who was an expert on stem cell research. She discussed the exciting prospect of adult stem cells, explaining that there was no need to destroy human embryos for research. Other couples then stood to share their embryo adoption stories, and at the end, a couple dedicated their little baby, Julian, who was the first baby born through Embryo Adoption Services of Cedar Park.

As Jason and I sat in the pew, I realized, in awe, that we were witnessing history. Not only was Julian the first baby to be born through the Cedar Park Embryo Adoption Services, but Cedar Park was the only church to have their very own embryo adoption service. As I watched the little baby wriggle and smile onstage, my heart leapt with joy again. *This could be us someday,* I realized.

After the service, we went to say hello to Maria. She gave us a hug and then asked, "Are you coming to lunch?"

Jason and I glanced at each other, unsure how to respond. We'd just met her, after all!

"It's across the parking lot. Just go on over, and I will be right behind you!" she said with a smile before leaving us.

"I dunno about this lunch," Jason told me hesitantly. "I was thinking we'd just check out the service and then head home to watch the Seahawks game and take a nap."

"Oh, it will be fun," I replied cheerfully, trying to drum up enthusiasm. I knew Jason got a bit nervous when meeting new people.

We walked in to discover six other people sitting at a table. We met Tom and his wife, Stacy, who was pregnant with Cedar Park's second embryo adoption baby. As we talked with them, we learned they went to our home church. We met another lady named Rachel, and she told us she and her husband were waiting to hear from a donor couple to see if they had been chosen as the recipients of their embryos. Lastly, we met Brian and Melanie, the parents of little Julian. Melanie was especially excited and upbeat as she introduced herself.

"I would love to mentor you through this process, if you want," she gushed. "You better contact me, and don't you think that I'm too busy or anything like that," she added with a smile.

The Heart of a Miracle

Then, to my amazement, she plopped little Julian right in my lap. I took in his precious little features — his adorable nose, his big eyes, his round cheeks, his soft head. *A living, breathing, healthy little baby who would not be here right now if it weren't for embryo adoption! This is amazing!*

"I know how painful and frustrating the infertility process can be," Melanie went on. "But this is your baby! Embryo adoption is a journey, and it is not always easy. It doesn't matter about the pain or the agony it takes to adopt that baby, because when you have that precious life in your arms, it will all be worthwhile."

Her words gave us hope. We were officially ready to embark on the embryo adoption journey.

The very next day, we turned in our application for the adoption. It included questions such as, "Why do you want to adopt?" and "Do you have a preferred ethnicity?" We carefully filled in each blank. Next, we completed an FBI and background check and underwent physical examinations. Finally, we did a home study to ensure our house would be a safe environment for our unborn child. Each step was similar to that of a traditional adoption. And with each completed process, I reminded myself that we were one step closer to having a child of our own.

That week, Jason and I began praying for our donor couple. We did not know them yet, but we knew they were out there somewhere — the genetic parents of our future children. I wondered where they were in the process. Did they have a baby already? Were they just starting in vitro fertilization? No matter the case, I knew they had a journey and a story of their own. Most likely, they, too, had known heartbreak. And though we'd never met, I already loved them.

On October 15, I underwent a surgery to open up my tubes. To our delight, our prayers were answered, and the surgery was successful. We continued a cycle of praying and waiting, praying and waiting. Early the following year, we learned that Jason was a candidate for a surgery that could possibly fix his infertility problem. The procedure was minimally invasive and covered by our insurance.

"The surgery could improve your sperm counts by 80 to 90 percent," the doctor told us.

The statistics sounded promising. Though our hearts were now devoted to embryo adoption, we wanted to remain open to the possibility that God could still work a miracle. If we were meant to conceive a child on our own, we believed it could happen. We decided to go through with Jason's surgery and see what happened.

The doctors informed us that we'd need to wait roughly three months before we found out for sure if the procedure had worked. On July 27, we learned that Jason's surgery had not been successful.

"I'm sorry, but the sperm counts have more than doubled in the wrong direction," the doctors said.

Instead of grieving, we felt only relief. We had surrendered our entire fertility process over to God, knowing he was in charge of it all. God had confirmed we were not able to conceive on our own, and we were okay with that. I had already fallen in love with the child or children we would adopt someday, and I did not want to forget them. Somewhere on a shelf sat our babies-to-be, just waiting for a chance at life.

"We have our answer," I told Jason. "And I feel completely at peace about everything."

Jason and I had been reading a book about adoption together. The book discussed how God had adopted each of us into his family and how, by adopting, we had a chance to show the world God's love. I had begun to see our infertility as a gift rather than a burden, a joy rather than a hardship. Though I knew there might be many more tears and challenges to come, I also knew this was the exact path God had asked us to walk down. He had led us to embryo adoption, and we could not wait to see where the journey led.

We shared about embryo adoption with our friends and family. Most of them, just like us, had never heard of it before. We explained the procedure and the details, and to our delight, they remained 100 percent supportive. They had watched us walk through the valley of grief, and their hearts had ached along with us. Now, they embraced our new adventure. We had all been given the wonderful gift of hope.

That summer, Jason and I put together an embryo adoption book, introducing our future donor couple to us. We included photos of our wedding, our travel adventures and our friends and family. I concluded the book with a brief letter to the couple.

Souls on Ice

Thank you for getting to know us. We are ready to turn the page and begin the next chapter of our family's story, and we pray that if our family and your family are God's match, we will move forward together in fulfilling God's will for these precious children.

Love, Jason and Kate

A few days later, Maria called us with news of a possible donor match. But the situation did not work out. We remained hopeful. On September 30, we received the most wonderful news we could have asked for. A second couple had reviewed our book and chosen us! We were elated.

Maria met with me at a diner for coffee and a visit not long after. As we sipped our coffee, she pulled a photo out and slid it across the table toward me.

"This is the couple's little boy. Your child's future biological brother," she said.

I picked up the picture and stared at it, incredulous. A gorgeous, smiling little boy stared back at me. I began to shake as I soaked up the photo, nearly ready to jump out of my seat with excitement. *This is tangible! This is real! And this is happening right now!*

When Jason returned home from work, I showed him the photo. "Isn't he adorable?" I gushed. "Our child could look like this someday!"

"Wow." Jason's eyes lit up. "Really amazing."

Our excitement mounted with each passing day. On October 19, we signed documents to make our adoption process official. In a wonderful, amazing and completely surprising way we never could have imagined in our wildest dreams, we were now on our way to becoming parents!

The Northwest air turned crisp as summer gave way to fall, and the leaves turned brilliant shades of orange and red. As Christmas approached, Jason and I decided to forgo the usual decorations on our tree and replace them with a variety of multi-colored snowflakes. Babies who were born from frozen embryos, we'd learned, were called snowflake babies. The snowflakes hung brightly on our tree, a reminder that by next year, we could possibly be strewing gifts for our new child beneath the branches.

On February 26, I began taking birth control pills and prenatal vitamins, preparing my body for my future pregnancy. A couple weeks later, I darted into Walgreens to grab my prenatal vitamins. The pharmacist informed me that they did not have any but told me he was happy to see if the store several minutes away had some in stock.

"That's okay," I replied, suddenly realizing that my appointment later that day was just a block away from the other store.

And then, in that moment, something wonderful and unforgettable happened. Clear as if he was standing at my side, God spoke to me. "Get ready," he said.

Get ready. Tears filled my eyes, as I knew beyond a shadow of a doubt that he had just whispered straight to my heart. *Get ready to embrace this journey. Get ready for the amazing things I have in store for you — things you* cannot even imagine right now. *Get ready for the ride of your life.*

I'm ready, God. I'm ready for the ride!

I began nightly Lupron injections the following week. Two weeks later, I decreased the Lupron injections from 10 to 5 units and began Vivelle estrogen patches. The doctors informed me that I needed to build up the lining of my uterus in order to prepare my body for the embryo transfer.

Every other day, I put on a new patch, starting at one and working myself up to four patches. The doctors had warned me that my hormones would change drastically, but nothing prepared me for the emotional rollercoaster I rode for the next few weeks.

After just one patch, I began snapping at Jason and crying uncontrollably. "What are you going to do when I'm up to four patches?" I asked him, half-laughing and half-crying.

"Roll out of bed onto the floor. And just keep rolling till I'm in the other room," he replied with a wry smile.

Oh, boy, I thought. *We're both in for it!*

I wrote another letter to our future babies, letting them know how excited I was to meet them.

Dear Sweet Peas,

We're coming to get you. This road has been long and hard and different than we ever could have imagined. But your daddy and I wouldn't change any of it for the world. We love you more than you could ever imagine. We've

The Heart of a Miracle

dreamed about you, talked about names for you and prayed for you. We want to be with you, we want to know you, to touch your baby soft skin, to hug you and to kiss you. You have a place in this world. You are known. You are loved. You are wanted. And you have been waited for … for a very long time. We're coming soon.

Love, Mommy and Daddy

Our pastor prayed for us and our unborn babies that week, asking God to guide our entire journey. That same week, I underwent an estrogen blood test and learned that my levels were just where they were supposed to be. I began acupuncture soon after, then began taking progesterone and an antibiotic.

By now, I'd become an expert at putting on and taking off my patches. Though I felt like a bit of a science experiment, I reminded myself that each procedure got us one step closer to meeting our future little baby boy or girl.

On April 13, we showed up at the doctor's office for our official embryo transfer. We'd dreamed of this day for so long, it was hard to believe it had arrived. As we prepared for the procedure, my mind wandered to my father, who'd sat at the foot of my bed every night when I was a child and told me stories. He'd woven many wonderful, imaginative tales, but my favorite was the one he told about me — about the day I was born. He and my mother had battled with infertility themselves, trying for 14 years to have children before conceiving me. When I was born via C-section, the nurse brought me around to my mother. The minute she saw me, tears began to stream down the sides of her face. My father's story was a beautiful reminder that I was loved, celebrated and very, very much wanted.

Jason and I had chosen to adopt five embryos and were willing to have all five children if it was meant to be. We had chosen to transfer two of the embryos for now and keep the three remaining embryos frozen until we were ready to have more children. Just as my parents had wanted and loved me, we already wanted and loved these unborn children with all our hearts. And now the big moment had finally arrived.

"The embryos have both survived the thaw," the doctor began. "I placed a tiny slit in each of the outer shells of the embryos to help break them out of their shells. They are viable and ready to be implanted."

The transfer went incredibly smoothly. Jason and I watched our embryos on the screen as they were placed into the catheter and inserted inside me.

"Ready, one, two, three! There they go!" the doctor announced.

Tears rolled down my cheeks as I absorbed the process, just as my mom had cried when she first saw me. I watched my stomach rising and falling on the ultrasound as I cried, hardly able to contain my joy. *This is the moment we have waited for, for so long. Everything is right with the world. They are home.* I instantly felt different. Though I could not feel them, I knew they were

The Heart of a Miracle

there — they were ours. And I was already protective of them.

Thank you, God, I prayed, humbled beyond belief. *Thank you that you have chosen us to be their mom and dad. Thank you for the chance at new life.*

We had to wait 10 days to get the blood test to confirm if I was pregnant or not. My parents flew out from New York in hopes of celebrating with us when we received the exciting news. I got the call while Jason was at work, so I waited until he could be with me to listen to the voicemail. We drove to a nearby park with a cliff overlooking the water below.

This is the most beautiful, perfect setting for this moment, I thought as we excitedly picked up the phone. *This is it! This is what we've been waiting for!*

And then came the words we were not prepared for, the words that hit us like an 18-wheeler moving at full speed. "I'm sorry, but the test came back negative. You are not pregnant."

Not pregnant. No, that can't be right! Everything went so well! I took all my medications, did everything the doctors told me to do! Surely, there must be some mistake!

Jason and I sat there, absorbing the blow, completely numb and in shock. The two babies we'd dreamed of, written letters to, picked out names for and prayed for … we'd lost them both. And there was nothing more we could do to save them.

We sat in the car in silence for a while, staring out at

Souls on Ice

the water below. Despite the serene setting, my insides were a tornado. *How, how, how?* Confusion and sadness overwhelmed me as I tried to make sense of everything. In anger, I ripped off my hormone patches. "What are we doing? Are we even supposed to have kids?" I screamed. "I don't know if we can keep doing this, Jason!"

Jason's face twisted into sadness; he was lost in his own grief. "I'll call your parents," he said quietly. "Tell them to give us some space when we get home."

When we returned home, I flew up to our bedroom and dove under the covers, never wanting to resurface again. *How, why, how, why?* I repeated all my questions to God as the tears came in a flood. We'd been so hopeful. We'd had no reason to believe the transfer would not work. We'd already gone through more than most couples would in a lifetime. We believed life began at conception, and we'd loved those frozen little embryos just as if they were two little people. Why would God take them from us?

We spent the next few days grieving. My parents and Jason's parents, having just lost their future grandchildren, grieved as well. This was supposed to be such a happy time for all of us, filled with baby shopping and celebration meals and laughter and hope. Now we were faced with an indescribable loss, and none of us knew what to do.

As the days passed, I realized I did not know quite how to grieve. Sometimes I swung into superficial mode, replying with a plastic smile and a perky, "I'm good, thanks for asking!" when people inquired about my state.

The Heart of a Miracle

Other days, I screamed and cried like a wild animal, barely recognizing myself. Discouraging thoughts began to fill my mind as bitterness, rage, jealousy and helplessness set in. *Why is it so easy for everyone else to have a baby, but our journey is so hard? This just isn't fair!*

Jason shared some Bible verses from Psalms that brought great comfort to me. I took all my grief to God, knowing he was grieving along with me. I surrendered it all to him — my dreams, my fears, my joy, my heartache. And I chose to trust in him. I knew that he saw our pain, that he cared and that he would deliver us from it. I also knew that our story was far from over. I ached to be a mother more than anything in the world. God knew that because he knew my heart. I could only rest in his promises and his love and leave the rest up to him.

In July, we spoke with Maria Lancaster and shared our struggles with her. She encouraged us to move forward with the second transfer. We were just about ready to leave for a camping trip to celebrate our wedding anniversary. Daring to hope and dream again, I called our doctor and asked him what he thought about us proceeding with the other three embryos.

"What day are you on in your monthly cycle?" he asked.

I told him, and he replied, "If you are on day six of your cycle, you should proceed right away."

Jason and I discussed the situation. We'd already had to take out a loan for the first embryo transfer, and finances had been tight.

Souls on Ice

"Maybe we should wait," I told him with a sigh.

We called the doctor back and told him we needed to wait until we got our finances in order. An hour later, I went to retrieve the mail and discovered a check from a family member in the exact amount we needed to complete the second transfer. We stared at the check, completely blown away by God's amazing timing.

"Wow! I guess we're going for it!" I squealed. We thanked God for his provision, thanked our family member for such overwhelming generosity and called the doctor back with our good news.

I picked up the necessary medications, and we went camping as planned. During our trip, we discussed what it would mean to transfer three embryos at once. All three embryos were frozen in one straw, so thawing and transferring the three that survived seemed to be the only option for us. There was a chance we could have triplets. Could we handle three babies at once? Our doctor told us that the embryos had the best shot at life by being thawed and transferred together. We prepared ourselves for the possible challenges that could come with having triplets. Each of the three little lives were precious to us, and we weren't going to do anything to put them at risk.

I proceeded with the hormone shots as before, and we began praying fervently, asking God to give us the desire of our hearts. On August 23, I underwent the second transfer and waited the requisite 10 days. I felt like a kid counting down the days until Christmas as we held our breath. On August 31, I picked up a home pregnancy test and took it. I had taken roughly 30 pregnancy tests since we'd first begun our journey, and each time the result had been the same. Would this one be different?

Please, God, please, I prayed as I anxiously waited for the results. And then, to my utter joy and amazement, I saw the faintest pink line show up on the stick. I started shaking as I grabbed my keys and hopped in the car. I headed straight for Jason's work.

I hid a camera just inside the door, so that when Jason got into our car thinking we were headed out to lunch, I could record his reaction.

"I'm pregnant!" I whispered in his ear across the console. "Really pregnant!"

"Are you sure?" Jason asked repeatedly, his eyes wide with disbelief.

The tears came. "I'm sure. This time, I'm sure." My heart surged with joy. God had answered our prayers! We were going to have a baby at last!

My parents flew in from New York again. When we got to the airport parking garage, we opened up the trunk, where we'd hidden a sign that read, "We are pregnant!" They jumped up and down, screaming excitedly and rejoicing with us. Finally, we all had a reason to celebrate. After enduring a long journey of pain, frustration and waiting, we were about to embark on a new journey, preparing for new life in our home and our hearts.

I got an official blood test the next day, and it came back positive. My hormone levels continued to rise, and we took it as a sign that all was going well. We still knew

Souls on Ice

there was a chance we could have twins or triplets if all three embryos survived, but only time would tell. In the meantime, we prayed that God would protect these precious little lives inside my belly.

On September 17, Jason took the first side-angle pregnancy photo of me. We planned to take one every week, documenting the pregnancy as my belly continued to grow. Suddenly, I felt a warm gush beneath my legs. I ran to the bathroom and discovered I was bleeding heavily. I didn't cry or yell — I simply went numb. *I'm miscarrying. I'm losing the babies.* Our short-lived joy disappeared as we braced ourselves for the inevitable. We were not going to be pregnant after all.

We called the doctor, and she told us we needed to come in for an emergency ultrasound first thing the following morning. The bleeding continued throughout the night. Jason and I lay in bed, crying and singing worship songs to Jesus. We asked him to prepare our hearts for the worst. Suddenly, I no longer felt pregnant. It was as if all my symptoms had disappeared with that gush. I was certain there was no way the baby, or babies, had survived.

I cried all the way into the doctor's office. When we learned we'd be seeing the doctor we'd been working with all along, a huge sigh of relief escaped me. *Thank you, God. You are kind.*

"Heavy bleeding?" the doctor asked quietly, noting my fallen face.

I nodded. "Super heavy. With at least five big clots."

The Heart of a Miracle

"Okay, well, I will be honest with you. I'll just say it like it is and not give you any false hope," he said.

"Okay," I whispered.

Jason held my hand as the doctor began the ultrasound. Moments later, the doctor exclaimed, "I have a heartbeat!"

"What?!" Jason cried, laughing out loud. "Are you serious?"

"Oh, my God; oh, my God," I cried out to God, unable to believe what I'd just heard. The same elation we'd felt when we saw the positive pregnancy test returned as we rejoiced in our little miracle. We had a baby after all!

"There's a second gestational sac here. You had a twin, and the sac is collapsing," the doctor went on. "That would explain the bleeding."

A million emotions flooded me at once. We had one healthy baby, but we'd lost another one at the same time. *Life and death simultaneously.* I pressed the doctor for more answers, wanting to make sure there was no chance the other baby had survived. But he grimly told me it was not a viable pregnancy.

"I'm sorry," he said sensitively.

I was grateful for his kindness. I knew he didn't take our situation lightly. He had ridden the rollercoaster with us since the beginning, and he wanted nothing more than to see us be parents. We continued to stare at the screen, watching our remaining baby's heart beat at a perfect 118 beats per minute. We grieved and we celebrated at the same time. It would be an unforgettable day, one that would stand out as one of the most joyous and most heartbreaking in our journey thus far.

I graduated from our endocrinologist to a regular obstetrician and continued to have regular visits. The doctor assured us that everything was proceeding as normal, and we rejoiced. Though fear continued to linger in the back of our minds, we continued to pray, trusting that God would bring this baby into the world safely. We knew we were not in control of anything, and we had no other choice but to give it all up to him. He was the author of life, and things would play out just as he wanted them to.

Around Thanksgiving, I felt the first strong movement from the baby in my belly. *This is real,* I thought joyously, marveling at the little life growing inside of me. *There is a real, developing baby in here!*

Christmastime rolled around, bringing with it another chilly Northwestern winter. In addition to celebrating Jesus' birthday, Jason and I now had another reason to celebrate. We had a baby on the way! We went out and picked up a crib and began setting up the nursery with my parents' help. We also began buying little clothes. By Christmas Day, the baby's room was nearly done, complete with bright hues of black, white, yellow and teal. At one point, I'd never dreamed I'd have the chance to do things like this. Now, it was all happening. With the nursery ready to go, it was time to sit back and wait for the baby to arrive.

The day after Christmas, I had an ultrasound to reveal

The Heart of a Miracle

the baby's gender. We asked the ultrasound tech to write down the sex and put it in an envelope. We then put together a gender reveal party for the next day and invited more than 100 of our closest friends and family. We made it fun with pictures, games and a big box that read, "Blue or pink, what do you think?" Inside the box, our friends had placed either pink or blue balloons after opening the envelope and finding out the gender themselves. When we opened the box, several blue balloons flew out. We were having a boy!

We had not hoped for a particular sex and were thrilled to learn we were having a boy. We'd already settled on the name Liam, with John being the middle name. Liam, I discovered, meant "protector," and John meant "God has been gracious." The meaning could not have been more perfect for our situation. God had truly been gracious.

On January 18, 2013, at 1 a.m., I felt a huge gush while lying in bed. We rushed to the hospital, where the doctors confirmed my water had indeed broken. They immediately began running tests, monitoring the fetal heartbeat and pumping in antibiotics and steroids. Anxiety set in as I realized that I was only 23 weeks along. Twenty-four weeks is considered viability, which meant I needed to hang in there a couple more days in order to give the baby a stronger chance of survival.

Statistically, I knew the situation was dire. Fifty percent of women go into labor within 48 hours of their water breaking, and 90 percent go into labor within a week. If Liam came before Monday, his chance of survival was as low as 10 percent with a 100 percent chance of serious birth defects. His chances improved with each passing day he waited to be born, but we were far from out of the woods. I'd thought we'd already jumped through the biggest hurdles in our pregnancy journey, but it turned out we were just about to face a whole new set of them.

Though the doctors remained concerned, they grew more optimistic with each passing day. I made it past 24 weeks and then into my 25th week. They kept me at the hospital on bed rest so they could closely monitor me and the baby. We contacted our friends and family and asked them to pray for us. As I lay in bed, watching Liam's little heartbeat on the monitor and feeling him move inside of me, I prayed, too, asking God to please complete our miracle. *Please, God, let this little boy live, and let him be healthy,* I pleaded.

"I can't believe you are still pregnant," the doctors and nurses said, incredulous as each day passed and still I did not go into labor. "This is truly amazing."

On March 2, nearly 30 weeks into my pregnancy, my blood pressure skyrocketed, and the doctors rushed me in for an emergency C-section.

"Jesus, I put Liam in your hands. I trust you with my son and with my life," I prayed, just before the doctors knocked me out.

When I awoke, super groggy and dazed, Jason wheeled me down to the Neonatal Intensive Care Unit, where I met our son for the very first time. Little Liam, weighing a

The Heart of a Miracle

mere 3 pounds, lay in an incubator, his tiny little body completely covered with tubes and wires. I stuck my finger into his Isolette and gripped his tiny little finger, unable to believe he was really here.

Our baby boy. The baby we've prayed about and dreamed about for so long. He's finally here! And I'm touching him right now! This is truly a miracle from God.

After two days, I got to hold Liam at last. He was so tiny that he fit between my chin and my chest as I ever so gently pressed him against my skin. We cuddled for more than an hour, and I counted all of his fingers and toes, marveling at his tiny but perfect features.

Dear Sweet Pea ... I thought of the letter I'd written two and a half years before to a baby I had yet to meet. We hadn't known where our journey would lead, all the peaks and valleys we'd walk through. We'd had no idea it would be so hard, that there would be so many tears and so much heartache involved. But right now, holding our little guy — our little miracle — I was reminded of God's faithfulness, his care and his love. Everything had led to this beautiful moment. It had all been worth it.

ఞఞఞ

There they are! This is the moment we've been waiting for! Lisa dropped her bag and ran toward me, her arms outstretched, as though we'd known each other all our lives. Tears filled her eyes as she released me from her embrace and smiled.

Souls on Ice

"It's so nice to meet you!" she gushed.

"You, too," I cried, tears pricking my own eyes. I shifted little Liam on my hip so that he faced her. "This is Liam John," I said.

Lisa and Mark were visiting Washington from the East Coast and had happily agreed to meet us at a local Seattle park on a hot and beautiful August afternoon. For the first time, we'd have a chance to introduce ourselves and Liam and thank them for the incredible gift of life they'd given us.

Since the beginning, Jason and I had hoped for an open adoption so that we could keep in contact with the donor family. We had prayed for them even before they'd selected us, and we knew they had been praying for us, too. It seemed surreal that we were all standing here at last, embracing and crying as our journeys came full circle.

Little Joshua, Lisa and Mark's 9-year-old son, held out a teddy bear he'd brought for Liam. I thanked him, and he excitedly explained that he'd just returned from summer karate camp. He jumped happily in the water spigots, and my heart warmed with joy. *Maybe this will be Liam someday,* I thought, taking in Joshua's wide smile, beautiful features and his bubbling enthusiasm.

We spent the day playing and chatting, just like old friends catching up. Lisa and Mark were even more wonderful than I'd imagined, and I thanked God once again for bringing them into our lives. As our day ended with more hugs and tears, I reflected once again on our amazing journeys. Though we'd both struggled with

The Heart of a Miracle

heartbreak and infertility, we now saw it all as an amazing gift. Had it not been for what we went through, little Joshua and Liam would not be sitting here with us. They were both miracles, a reminder of God's faithfulness and love. Through the unique embryo adoption process, we'd had the opportunity to witness life from the very first stages. We'd seen an embryo turn into a beating heart, a swelling belly and then a beautiful blue-eyed child. God had taken our heartbreak and turned it into joy.

Perhaps there were more Liams out there, just waiting for a chance at life. Perhaps there was another family, wondering if they'd ever hold a little pink or blue bundle in their arms. Perhaps they, too, would discover the wonderful gift of embryo adoption and embrace it. Perhaps our story would play a part in theirs someday. After all, God had written our story, and though it had not played out like we'd imagined, we now knew that we'd never have it any other way.

> "Love you, O Lord, my strength. The Lord is my rock and my fortress and my deliverer, my God, my rock, in whom I take refuge, my shield, and the horn of my salvation, my stronghold. I call upon the Lord, who is worthy to be praised, and I am saved from my enemies." (Psalm 18:1-3 ESV)

Souls on Ice

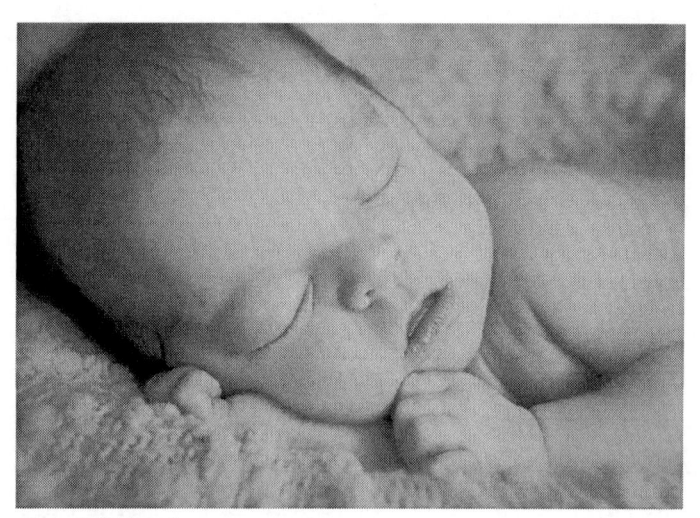

Liam McKenzie

Jason and Kate, holding their son, Liam

The Heart of a Miracle

Jason, Kate and Liam McKenzie

Joshua, Mark, Liam, Jason, Kate and Lisa, meeting each other in a park for the first time.

Hypothetical Utopia
The Adoption Story of Allen and Dañnette
Written by Arlene Showalter

"Hi, my name is Allen." I greeted each of the other teens as they stepped on the bus for our mission trip, while keeping an eye on the cute girl near the end of the line.

"Hi, I'm Allen." I leaned in and kissed her cheek.

She drew back. *Oops. Maybe my New Orleans culture doesn't fly in West Texas.* My cheeks burned as I scrambled to clean up the mess I'd made.

"Just a holy kiss," I stammered. "Like the Bible says: 'Greet one another with a holy kiss.'"

I admired her olive-toned skin and humongous brown eyes, even though I knew I was the target of the annoyance shining in them. She boarded the bus without a word.

As we settled in our seats, I made sure I sat close by her. I half-listened to the girls' chatter as we drove deep into Mexico. *I want to get to know that beautiful girl sitting two rows back.*

Some of the kids began discussing what they wanted to do with their lives. I already knew the direction I would take. At 13, I'd felt God calling me to be a missionary or a pastor, and even though I was still only 15, I knew the importance of choosing the right wife for my life's work.

"I want to be a pastor's wife," I heard one girl say. My

radar picked up her signal. I tried to look blasé as I turned to see who spoke. *Cute Girl in parking lot.* My heart skipped.

At that moment, she pulled out her hair scrunchie and shook her long, dark curls loose. *She has the right heart, and she's gorgeous, too.* My heart galloped.

We spent a week in Mexico, sharing God's love with the locals and ministering to children. We teens also helped by going door to door every morning, inviting people to the evening services.

Because of my fluency in Spanish, I was tagged as one of the interpreters, making sure to be in Dannette's group every time.

I floated through the week. *Here I am,* I thought, *on this mission trip, working side by side with this beautiful girl, and she feels called to be a pastor's wife ... we're actually doing ministry together!*

Our last day in Mexico came, and we prepared to return to the States. *She already has my heart, but she doesn't act in the least bit interested in me. And I think she realizes that I'm interested in her. What can I do? I have to do something. I may never see her again.*

I drew Dannette to one side just before she boarded the bus.

"In a hypothetical utopia," I began, avoiding the now-familiar expression of irritation on her pretty face, "you and I would be together."

She flicked her doe eyes over me, the short 5-foot, 7-inch Cajun kid, and said, "I don't even know what that

Hypothetical Utopia

means, but if I *did* know what it means, Tom Cruise and I would be together, not you and I."

"Well … I really like you. Can I write to you, anyway?"

&&&

When Allen asked for my address, I thought, *What's the harm? We live 900 miles apart. He'll write a few times and tire of it.* I shrugged and gave it to him.

His letters arrived before I could forget his existence. Not mushy ones filled with longings or feelings, but rather pages and pages of lengthy theological discourses. I staggered through each volume with rolling eyes and then set out to "answer" them, dashing off my typical reply: *I'm doing well. I'm going to school. I have a boyfriend. Have a nice day. Dannette.*

The next year, I graduated high school and enrolled in the local community college before my 17th birthday.

"I wish you'd stop bothering me," I groaned when another missive arrived. After a year of my complete lack of interest, his letters gradually slowed from a flood to a trickle. "Maybe he finally gets it."

Two years after we'd met, Allen called me in December of 1998. "I've known your pastor, Billy, for years, and he invited me to come for a six-month internship at your church," he said.

"That's nice." My voice remained as flat as my feelings.

"He suggested I take some classes at MC," Allen continued. "Is that where you go?"

"Yes." I rolled my eyes heavenward.

"Can you tell me which professors to avoid?"

"Sure." *But I won't tell you what classes I'm taking. The last thing I need is you following me around campus like a puppy dog.*

The first day of school, I walked into my Anatomy & Physiology class. Allen sat in the second row.

You've got to be kidding, I thought, while maintaining a polite smile. *Of all the A&P classes offered, he ends up in mine. That's funny, God. Real funny.*

Mom heard me crying in my room a few months later and popped her head in the door.

"Mi hija," she said, "what's wrong?"

"God's going to make me marry Allen."

"What?"

"I just know God's going to make me marry him."

"God won't make you do something you don't want to do," she said gently, sitting beside me on the bed.

"I think he will. I'm not attracted to him," I sobbed. "And besides, he wants to be a missionary in Mexico. I am not interested in that."

"You've got nothing to worry about," Mom said. "You can't date before you're 18, anyway."

For the first time in my life, I thanked God for my parents' strict outlook on the subject.

Even though Allen failed to interest me in any way at first, I began to see his heart and how much he loved the

Hypothetical Utopia

Lord. With infinite, gentle patience, God started working in my own heart.

One day, before class started, Allen and I had a long talk.

"I think the Lord is calling me to marry you," he said. "I know you don't feel the same way, but just take that thought and pray about it."

"I already know I'm supposed to marry you," I said, clutching my books to my chest like a shield. "I just don't want to."

"That's okay," Allen said. His face lit up like a Texas-sized harvest moon. "We can work on that part!"

Allen's parents evidently were already on board about me, based on whatever he'd told them, but my parents needed a bit more convincing about him.

"We'll let you date," Mom said, "but only within a group. He can come to our family gatherings."

"And church events," Dad added.

Maybe he's not so bad, I thought as I continued to study his heart. *He loves God so much and has such a passion for other people.* My own heart began to respond, first with admiration, then fondness that inched forward into full-blown love. *I would be honored to be his wife,* I thought, while wondering, *How could I not see what a catch this guy is?*

☙☙☙

Souls on Ice

I visited Dannette's parents, alone, in August of 2000.

"You know I love your daughter," I said. "And I want to marry her. I would like to ask for your permission and blessing to marry her."

"We know you are a good man and will treat her right. And she loves you, too. You have my blessing."

"I want her to come and meet my family during the holidays," I said. "I'd like to propose to her on a riverboat cruise."

"Sounds great," her dad said.

"So romantic," her mom sighed.

"I booked a cruise for New Year's Eve," I told Dannette after she flew to New Orleans. "A sunset dinner cruise on the Natchez Steamboat."

"Oh, that sounds wonderful," she said.

We floated down the Mississippi, listening to the *thwap, thwap, thwap* of the boat's paddlewheel.

After a delicious Cajun dinner, a Dixieland band struck up, playing good New Orleans-style jazz. I led Dannette to the top deck, and we watched the sun sink in the west.

We had the deck to ourselves.

"Dannette," I said, taking her hand. "Will you marry me?"

"Yes, yes," she said, jumping up and down. Then she stopped when she saw the ring I held out.

"Do my parents know?" she asked. "Are they okay with this?"

Hypothetical Utopia

"Talked to them back in August," I said, grinning. "They're fine with it."

We celebrated New Year's Day 2001 engaged — and married six months later.

❧❧❧

Allen and I were both 20 when we married, so we decided to wait about five years to start a family, giving us time to settle into the marriage and save money to buy a house. I worked at an aquatics center, and Allen worked as a registered nurse at the local hospital.

I underwent bladder surgery at 22. Memories of female problems in my teen years came back.

"What if, when we're ready to start a family, I can't have kids?" I'd ask Allen.

"There's no way the Lord would give you such a desire for children," Allen said, "and not give you the ability. I've seen the way you are around kids." A gentle smile tugged at his lips. "I've always found your love for children very attractive. If anyone was born to be a mother, she's you."

"You're right about that," I said. "All I've ever wanted was to be a mommy."

❧❧❧

We followed through with our plan and began trying to have a family when we were 25. After eight months, we decided it would be best for Dannette to visit her gynecologist.

"I thought you might have a problem conceiving," Dr. Smith said, "at the time of your bladder surgery. Let's start monitoring your cycle. I'll also give you a prescription for progesterone to help you ovulate."

A year passed. "I'm sorry," Dr. Smith said, "but I can't do anything else for you. You'll have to go see a specialist."

I saw the devastation in my wife's eyes. We drove home in silence. I knew Dannette's thoughts. They echoed my own.

All our friends are either pregnant or already have their first child. We're the only ones left out.

I felt her sorrow, because her sorrow was my sorrow, and I could do nothing to relieve her of her pain.

The need to consult with a fertility doctor forced me to come to terms with the fact that we wouldn't be able to conceive a child on our own. *How can this be God's plan?* I wondered over and over again.

"Maybe going to a fertility specialist is God's plan for us," Dannette said. "Who are we to question how he chooses to give us children?"

"You're right." *Who am I to question your ways, Lord?*

We made an appointment with Dr. Sarah. Hope returned.

"Let's start you out on medications to get you ovulating," Dr. Sarah said, "and we'll monitor your natural cycle."

"I feel better now," I told Dannette on our way home. "Maybe this will really help."

Hope brightened and dimmed every 30 days as each

pregnancy test came back negative. Six tests later, we returned to Dr. Sarah.

"I've studied your latest exams," Dr. Sarah said, "and I doubt you two can ever get pregnant the conventional way."

"Why not?" Dañnette asked.

"Because your uterus is folded over, and you may have endometriosis." She laid Dañnette's chart down and folded her hands over it. "We can try IUI — intrauterine insemination."

Dañnette and I exchanged glances.

"We'll do it," I said.

Dañnette's eyes glowed as she underwent the procedure.

My heart thumped. We went home and waited for the phone call confirming we were nine months from parenthood.

The phone rang. Dañnette pressed the button for speakerphone. "I'm so sorry." The nurse's voice was filled with compassion. "You're not pregnant."

Dañnette dropped the phone and looked at me. "I feel like I've been punched in the gut," she sobbed, rubbing her vacant stomach. Then her brown eyes snapped. "How can God do this to us?" she cried. "How?"

I watched my wife's hopes and dreams come dashing to the ground. Her whole world was falling apart. Her future — our future — seemed to be shattering to pieces. I wanted more than anything to gather up those pieces and put them back together. I wanted to assure her that everything was going to be okay, but I couldn't. My own heart seemed to be lost somewhere in that pile of broken dreams and shattered hopes.

What can I do? What can I say? I'm hurting as bad as she is. I need to be strong for her, but how can I be when I'm as devastated as she?

"Call Pastor Billy," Dañnette said. "I can't take this."

I called. Pastor Billy, who's known both of us most of our lives, is like a father to us, even calling us his son and daughter.

"Come right over," he said.

"It's not fair," Dañnette cried as Pastor Billy hugged her. "Why would God give all our friends babies, and some of them had problems conceiving as well, and not us?" She sobbed in Pastor Billy's arms. "It's just not fair."

After Dañnette calmed down a little, Pastor Billy pointed to some chairs. "Have a seat," he said as he reached for his Bible.

"Listen to the prayer of Asaph in Psalm 73: 'Surely God is good … to those who are pure in heart. But as for me, my feet had almost slipped; I had nearly lost my foothold. For I envied the arrogant when I saw the prosperity of the wicked. They have no struggles; their bodies are healthy and strong. They are free from the burdens common to man; they are not plagued by human ills … When I tried to understand all this, it was oppressive to me till I entered the sanctuary of God; then I understood their final destiny. Yet I am always with you; you hold me by my right hand … My flesh and my heart may fail, but God is the strength of my heart … as for me, it is good to be near God. I have made the Sovereign Lord my refuge.'"

He leaned forward and touched Dannette's hand. "It's okay to be honest with God," he said. "He can handle your anger. Just don't stay in that place. Look at Asaph, how upset he was *until* he went into God's presence. There, he found hope."

❧❧❧

"It looks like you need a polypectomy, Dannette," Dr. Sarah said, studying my latest exam reports. "It appears you have a polyp, a small skin growth, at the top of your uterus. It needs to come out because it can hinder embryo implantation."

"Do you think that's why the IUI failed?" Allen asked.

"Quite possibly," Dr. Sarah said.

"Let's do it," I said.

After the procedure, she scheduled another IUI.

We waited. We prayed. We hoped.

Then my period came. Another period. Another failure.

I had two additional polypectomies because the same polyp grew back, with IUI procedures after each.

We waited. We prayed. We hoped.

Two more negatives.

"I'm going to schedule a laparoscopy," Dr. Sarah said. "It's a procedure in which a small lighted tube is inserted through your belly button to check for endometriosis." I was in stage three, which is fairly advanced, but the doctor was able to remedy the problem.

Hope flagged but recovered.

Two more IUIs.

Two more negatives.

"I'm done," I cried, after another failed IUI. "I can't take this anymore."

"Let's keep trying," Allen encouraged. "What if it works the next time and we miss out because we quit? Surely, we're making progress as Dr. Sarah finds and fixes these other problems that seem to be blocking conception."

"You're right," I sobbed. "Maybe next time."

༄༄༄

"Dannette, listen to this!" I could hardly contain my excitement when I called my wife on the phone.

"What is it?" she asked.

"I'm reading this article in Focus on the Family," I said. "Have you ever heard of snowflake babies?"

"Snowflake what?" she asked.

"Snowflake babies," I repeated.

"Never heard of it," Dannette said. "It sounds a little weird."

"Couples who have remaining embryos after they go through the process of in vitro fertilization sometimes put their embryos up for adoption for people who can't conceive their own kids," I said. "They call them snowflake babies. Maybe we should research it."

"Maybe. It does sound intriguing." She hesitated. "Let's see if Dr. Sarah can help us get our own baby first. We could look into that later."

We continued with the seventh IUI.

"God, help us," I cried over and over again as I watched Dannette's agony. I held her as she wept, helpless to give her the one thing we both desired.

"God is in sovereign control," I reminded Dannette and myself a million times. "Remember Asaph's prayer in Psalm 73." Meanwhile, my spirit sagged. *We'd better not be NOT able to have kids.*

"This must be God's will," I said, while wondering where his goodness lay in all our agony. "Think how much we will appreciate our baby when he or she finally comes. God is with us in the midst of our sufferings. And we will be able to encourage other couples in the future who will go through the same disappointments."

I hid my own pain. "God," I prayed, staring out the window at nothing. "I know — we know — that you are sovereign, you have everything under control. You knew this day would come before either of us was born. You knew us before the foundation of the world. We get that. But how … how are you good right now? How is this struggle good for us?"

Our friends continued growing their own families, while we grappled with more negative test results.

"I ran into someone today," Dannette said some months later. "The woman's adopted several children. We got to talking, and I mentioned what you told me about embryo adoption." She got up to start cooking dinner. "What did you call those babies?"

"Snowflake."

Dannette giggled — a welcome sound in our house.

"I suppose that's because the embryos are frozen," I said, "and each one is unique, like a snowflake."

"She told me she's considered that route for herself," Dannette continued. "Maybe we ought to research it ourselves."

We continued with the tweaks and IUIs. The results never changed. Finally, we decided to tell Dr. Sarah our thoughts.

"We've been thinking about embryo adoption," Dannette told her.

"I think it's a great idea," Dr. Sarah said. She smiled. "In fact, I have embryos stored, right this minute, in my lab. Maybe we could use one of those if another IUI fails."

"Let's try one more IUI," I said. "We'll decide on embryo adoption later."

I saw the fatigue on Dannette's face and in her large dovelike brown eyes.

"It's your body, honey," I said. "You have to decide on whether or not to stop trying. Do you want to go for an eighth IUI or move on to adoption?"

"I'm done," Dannette said. "Let's look into all types of adoption. The idea has always been in the back of my

Hypothetical Utopia

mind." Her eyes teared up. "Think of the one-child law in China. Or other kids considered unadoptable. Maybe God wants us to give one of them a home."

"You are a shield around me, O Lord," Dañnette read from Psalm 103, "you bestow glory on me and lift up my head. To the Lord I cry aloud, and he answers me … I lie down and sleep; I wake again, because the Lord sustains me … Deliver me, O my God … From the Lord comes deliverance."

Together, we mourned the death of our dreams and the children who never came to be.

We found a Web site that listed different agencies offering embryo adoption, and I contacted every single one of them. Most responded in a week or so with a general, impersonal e-mail.

Maria of Embryo Adoption Services called me a few hours after my initial e-mail.

"I got your e-mail," she said over the phone. "I'm here to serve you."

The responses from other agencies trickled in, and Dañnette and I discussed each one. We kept coming back to Maria, partly because the ministry was based in a church.

"Let's check out the church Web site," I suggested.

"Good idea," Dañnette agreed.

We clicked on the site and watched an hour-long video.

241

Souls on Ice

The pastor, Dr. Joseph Fuiten, spoke, and then Maria spoke about her own embryo adoption story.

"I like this organization," Dannette said. "They're very faith-based."

"I agree," I said. "I think this is the right agency for us. Let's go with them. I'll call Maria back."

"We're ready," I told her. "Let's do this."

"Wonderful," she said. "I'll send you the paperwork."

After we completed that, Maria called us.

"I've scheduled a home study," she said. "You'll love our social worker, Heather. She goes to all the prospective parents' homes for our organization."

The day of the home study came. We called our parents and closest friends.

"Please pray for us," we begged. "We're being evaluated today to see if we qualify for a baby."

"You'll be fine," they all agreed.

Heather came in November of 2011, and her quiet, compassionate demeanor relaxed us within minutes. We conversed for several hours, then she prayed with us and left.

Maria called three weeks later. "You're approved," she said. "Are you ready for the next step?"

"Yes, we are!"

We filed more paperwork, including a photo book for the prospective donor family, who had to approve the match. Since we were a biracial couple, Maria counseled us that it could take a while to find Hispanic and Caucasian embryos.

Hypothetical Utopia

"God has a funny way of connecting the right families so the born children look like their parents," she explained. "This part of the matching process could take a little longer, but we want to be sure and pray over this match in order to find just the right donor family."

We sent out our photo book in January of 2012 — and waited.

"I feel like I'm on pins and needles," Dannette said. "Do you think the donor family will like us? How long will it take?"

"She said it could take up to a year," I reminded my lovely wife, trying to be gentle.

Several months passed. We waited.

"Nobody likes us," Dannette sobbed.

☙☙☙

Four months after our final paperwork was completed, Allen looked up from the computer. "We got *the* e-mail from Maria."

I raced over to his side and bent down to read it with him.

I think we have a match! Maria had written.

"A match. A match!" I squealed. Allen jumped up and grabbed my hands. We danced around the room, while I chanted, "A match. We've got a match."

We settled down enough to e-mail Maria back, asking for more information. She sent us a picture and a brief description of the donor family.

Souls on Ice

I stared at the photo of the donor mom and her twin girls smiling into the camera.

"Oh, Allen," I said, "they are so adorable."

"Let's get more information," he said.

We learned the family had only one available embryo. My heart dropped.

"Only one?" I rubbed my arms. "What if it doesn't take?"

"Let's go with it," Allen said.

"But what if it doesn't take?" I repeated. "We'd have to do it all over again. I don't know if I can do it again."

"It'll take," Allen said.

"But you know the stats," I said. "Only 35 percent success rate per transfer. Maybe we should wait for a donor family with more embryos to adopt."

"How can we not do this?" Allen asked. "If this is the baby God has chosen for us, how can we not give it a chance at life? Isn't this one baby worth the chance?"

"You're right," I agreed. "One life is worth the chance."

"It's a step of faith," Allen said, "to trust God to give us a baby with so little to work with."

I knew he was right. "Whether we have a live baby or God takes the baby home to heaven, at least we got the soul out of the freezer and gave him or her a chance at life."

A month later, in the quiet of night, I wrote in my prayer journal.

Hypothetical Utopia

May 17, 2012. Grateful for a match! Yet sad and afraid. Sad, for this means our biological child won't be our first and afraid we may lose our adopted child before we know him/her. Fear is reigning, but I need you to reign, Father, over my heart, over Allen's heart, be bigger than our fears. Read Mark 4:38-41 — "Why are you so afraid? Have you still no faith? And they were filled with great fear ..." Replace my fear with fear of you, Lord. I trust your heart, I trust your name.

Meanwhile, our dearly loved Dr. Sarah retired, and the doctor who took over her practice wasn't equipped to do an embryo transfer because their lab was not yet ready. We waited several more months and then contacted Maria with our dilemma.

"Let me call the clinic where this embryo was created," she said. "I know the doctor there. Perhaps she will agree to do the procedure for you."

"Good news!" Maria told us later. "Dr. Klein has agreed to help you. She can see you in two weeks."

We booked a flight from Texas to Seattle and met Dr. Nancy Klein. She instructed me on how to prepare my body for pregnancy, prescribed the necessary meds and arranged for my local doctors to monitor me.

"We'll target November 7 as your transfer date," Dr. Klein told us. She smiled. "How does that sound to you?"

Allen and I looked at each other. *Can it be so?* He smiled at me. *At last, at long last, we may actually get the desire of our heart?*

Souls on Ice

"We want you to be completely relaxed when you arrive for the procedure," Dr. Klein continued.

"How about a trip to Montana?" Allen suggested.

Montana! *My most favorite place on the earth.* "Yes," I agreed. "That would be a wonderful place to go to relax."

We flew up several days before our target date and rented a cabin on Flathead Lake. We hiked in Glacier National Park and drank in the beauty of God's handiwork.

"I love this baby already," I said.

"So do I," Allen agreed.

"What if ..."

I began to tell him all of the uncertainties and unknowns that were troubling me. Allen listened to my fears intently. "The boundary lines have fallen for me in pleasant places; surely I have a delightful inheritance," he quoted from Psalm 16. "I will praise the Lord, who counsels me; even at night my heart instructs me. I have set the Lord always before me. Because he is at my right hand, I will not be shaken."

I breathed deep of the crisp, pure air.

"I will be glad and rejoice in your love, for you saw my affliction and knew the anguish of my soul," I said. "Be merciful to me, O Lord, for I am in distress; my eyes grow weak with sorrow, my soul and my body with grief ... My life is consumed by anguish and my years by groaning; my strength fails because of my affliction, and my bones grow weak."

"Psalm 31." Allen grinned.

Hypothetical Utopia

"I'm thinking those years might be behind us now."

"Whatever happens," I told Allen, "we've given this baby a chance, and he or she will be living, either here with us or in heaven."

"I feel the same way," he said. "This baby is already ours, but the battle with infertility really isn't over until we hold him in our arms."

"Surely God wouldn't bring us this far just to let us down?"

"The Lord already knows what will happen. We're already so attached to this one baby, but we have to wait and see."

"Oh, man, this will be so bad if it doesn't work."

"Let's not borrow trouble," Allen said. "Let's read some of those letters again." Our church had put together a notebook, filled with encouraging letters from friends and family. We pored over them again and again up there in the mountains.

Allen picked up the book and rifled through the pages. "I am so pleased with the wisdom of God as he sent you into this snowflake adventure," he read. "I know that you have the grit and the power, graces from God, to match the task he has assigned to you. I recognize that it is not an ordinary project, but requires faith and courage and endurance which most people have no experience with. I also know that our God does not play post-modern power games but is a spring of living water. Your resources are not static, and your capacities for kindness and affection and peace are not fixed. ~Becca."

Souls on Ice

"Snowflake adventure," I repeated. "Our friends are just too precious."

We drove on to Seattle, a bit apprehensive, yet hopeful, and checked into a nearby motel where the clinic would call to tell us whether our baby had survived the thaw or not. The transfer appointment would be scheduled as soon as we found out.

The clinic called around noon.

"Your baby looks great," the nurse said, "so we're all set! We'll see you at 3:30 this afternoon. Make sure you're on time."

We laughed. "As if that's a problem," Allen said. "We've made it past the first hurdle." He grinned. "A successful thaw."

༄༄༄

Dannette and I were so excited that we left early to get to the appointment. "Just in case we can't find the clinic," we told ourselves. With more than two hours to spare, we decided to eat at a Chinese restaurant across the street. We enjoyed the quiet atmosphere and relaxed as much as humanly possible with so much at stake.

Our appointment time finally came. We re-crossed the street and, after being ushered into the room, met our team.

"I've been with your baby all morning," the embryologist said, smiling. "He or she survived the defrost process beautifully and appears very strong and healthy."

"How long did the thaw take?" I asked.

"It takes eight hours," she said. "I monitor the embryo under a microscope during that time to see how it is developing."

She pointed to a screen. "There," she said. "That's your baby right there."

"Wow," I said to Dannette. "We get to see our baby at five days old, as a microscopic embryo. How cool is that!"

"Most people don't get to see their baby for the first time until an ultrasound at six weeks."

As a nurse myself, I peppered the nurse with questions. "How can you know the baby won't get stuck in the syringe?" I asked. "How do you know the implantation is successful? That the baby makes it to the proper place?"

She smiled and waved her hand toward the screen. "Not to worry, Allen," she said. "You'll see the entire process right here."

I sat next to Dannette and took her hand, our eyes glued to that magical screen. We watched the point of the needle enter the fluid and saw the tiny bubble — our child — float into it.

Before the appointment, Dannette had been instructed to drink 20 ounces of water. Because of her folded uterus, Dr. Klein had to go in and unfold it, pressing against her overfilled bladder.

"I hope I don't pee on you," she said. "Either from pressure or excitement."

"Just hold it," she said, chuckling.

"This is just too amazing," I said, as we continued watching the screen. "That microscopic bubble is already a real human soul."

"God created this tiny life," Dannette said, "and we get to watch it grow."

"Most people never get to see this," I said, as we watched the progress over the screen.

Tears flowed from us as we tasted joy.

"God brought us to this point to experience this special event."

We returned to Texas two days later.

"I'm pregnant right now," Dannette said, as we drove home from the airport. "No matter what happens next, there's a baby inside me right now."

We waited for the two weeks to crawl by at snail speed to take the blood pregnancy test. Dannette kept holding on to that one thought, "No matter what happens, I've been pregnant for two weeks. I have a baby in me now."

Finally the day arrived. I took the day off. After seven years of infertility treatments, I'd learned that work and anticipation didn't mix.

I drove Dannette to the lab early in the morning. Even though the test was in Texas, that lab was to call Seattle with our results, and Dr. Klein would then contact us with the news sometime in the afternoon.

Around 10 a.m., Dannette realized she'd forgotten to give the Texas lab some information, so she called. Angelica, the nurse who'd worked with Dr. Sarah and had known us for years, answered. "I know I'm supposed to call Seattle first," she told Dannette, "but I have the results."

"Hold on," Dannette interrupted, "I want to put you on speakerphone so Allen can hear as well."

"I've known you for so long," she continued, after Dannette pressed the button for me to hear the news. "I just wanted to be the one to tell you myself."

"Okay," Dannette said. I watched her inhale and brace herself.

"Dannette," Angelica said, "you're pregnant!"

Tears slid down Dannette's face. "It worked," she whispered.

I burst out in tears.

"Are you kidding?" I said.

"We're pregnant?" Dannette asked.

"Now, make sure you act surprised when the Seattle office calls," Angelica said.

We spent the next hour crying, praying and thanking God. Years of pain, disappointment and heartache evaporated in that one moment.

Next, I called my family in New Orleans.

"Let's surprise our friends and family here," Dannette suggested. We jumped in our car and drove around all day, delivering our wonderful news to tears, screams of joy and thankfulness.

I drove Dannette to our first ultrasound appointment at seven weeks. She fidgeted beside me.

"I know the Lord gave us this baby," she said, "but what if he takes it away?"

The technician ushered us back into the room, and Dañnette lay on the table. I saw her hold her breath when the screen flipped on.

"There's your baby," she said, pointing. "Right there."

Our little "peanut baby," I thought. We stared at the one tiny, blinking pixel on the screen.

"And there's the heartbeat."

Dañnette released her breath. "That's the most beautiful sound I've ever heard," she sobbed.

&&&

Because of my previous bladder issues, the doctor scheduled a Cesarean section delivery for July 19, when I reached my 39th week.

On my birthday, July 16, I puttered around the house, working as my belly allowed.

"My back hurts so badly," I told Allen.

"Do you think you're having contractions?" he asked.

"No, I've been having hip and back pain for weeks," I said. "It's probably the same, just worse."

"Maybe you'd better lie down," he said.

That night I awakened at 3:45 a.m. *Yuck,* I thought, feeling the sheet beneath me. *Did I just pee the bed? Or ...*

I turned over and shook Allen awake.

"I think my water just broke."

"Well," he mumbled, "go to the bathroom and see."

Hypothetical Utopia

"I'm pretty sure my water broke!" I called out. "The baby's not supposed to come until the 19th. What am I going to do?"

"Don't worry," Allen said. His calm tone soothed me. "Everything's going to be fine. You call the doctor, and I'll pack the car."

I grabbed the suitcase that had stood packed and ready for two weeks. Allen slid behind the wheel. "God is with us," he said. "Don't worry."

I called my parents. "I think my water just broke," I said. "We're on our way to the hospital now."

We arrived around 5 a.m. "Yes, your water broke," the nurse confirmed. "The doctor will proceed with the C-section in an hour."

❧❧❧

They wheeled my wife down the hall while I paced the halls, waiting for the team to prep her for surgery. "Can I go in?" I'd asked the doctor.

"Sure," he said, "as long as you don't pass out."

"I'll be fine," I said. "I'm a nurse. Blood doesn't bother me."

As soon as they let me in the room, I sat next to Dannette. A curtain blocked our view of the procedure. Excitement and curiosity made me jump to my feet to peek over it.

"Come back down here with me," Dannette said, tugging on my hand.

Souls on Ice

I sat down. "Let me know when he's about to be born," I told the nurse. A little while later, she tapped me on the shoulder, and I popped up again.

I saw our baby boy's wet, black-haired head for the first time. The doctor leaned in to suction him, and he let out a huge cry, screaming the whole time the nurse cleaned him up and swaddled him. But the moment she put him in my arms, he stopped. I gazed down at this baby. *Perfect in every way.*

Then I bent down and placed him next to my wife's head. We both sobbed our relief and joy.

I straightened to study Dannette and our son. *We are finally out of our season of profound sadness. Lord, you have finally given us what we have asked for.*

As the doctor closed up Dannette's belly, he turned to me. "Tell everyone here your story," he said. "Tell them how this was an embryo adoption."

Dannette and I shared our journey, and then I left to tell our pastor, waiting in another room, our glorious news.

Shift change is at 7 a.m. As I passed the nurses' station, both night and day shift nurses huddled around our doctor as he told them about us and how our baby came to be.

In a hypothetical utopia, I thought, *Dannette and I would have had as many babies as quickly as we wanted. We had to fight as hard for this one as I had to fight for her love.*

My heart leapt in thankfulness to our perfect God. I

Hypothetical Utopia

knew that the Bible verse Psalm 30:5 read, "Weeping may last through the night, but joy comes with the morning." As we held our son in our arms for the first time, our years-long night of weeping over infertility had changed into a bright morning of joy.

"The LORD is my chosen portion and my cup; you hold my lot.
The lines have fallen for me in pleasant places; indeed,
I have a beautiful inheritance." (Psalm 16:4-6 ESV)

Allen and Dannette proudly holding
their newborn son

Miracles, a Country Apart
The Donating Story of Paul and Linda
Written by Joy Steiner Moore

My heart beat wildly as I skipped up the steps to our porch and swung open our front door.

"Paul?"

"I'm in here!" my husband called from the direction of his home office.

When I entered the room, Paul sat casually behind his desk typing on his computer. I took a deep breath. I had envisioned this moment so many times over the years — in a hundred different ways, in many different places and in every season. I had seen it next to the Christmas tree, on a vacation, on the beach. But it was happening now, in January 2007, in my husband's office. This was the moment I had dreamed of, and suddenly it didn't matter where we were.

"Why are you home so early?" he asked, glancing up from his work.

"I have something to show you." I reached into my purse and pulled out the pregnancy test, holding it out for him to see. "It's positive."

Paul's mouth dropped open in disbelief.

"You're kidding."

"No, I'm not. I took the test at work." I beamed.

Souls on Ice

After three years of infertility treatments and thousands and thousands of dollars spent, we'd been taking a break from actively "trying" to have a baby. We had exhausted both our resources and my body. And now, after all the fertility practices we'd tried — the medicine, the injections, the procedures and the methods — it had happened completely naturally, all on its own. It was truly unbelievable.

Paul didn't seem to know what to say. His brow furrowed with skepticism and concern.

"I need some time to process this. I think I'll go to the gym," he said, grabbing his workout bag from its hook. "Can we take another test?"

"These tests don't lie, Paul. This is real."

I knew my husband well, and I understood that after so much disappointment, he was cautious about getting too excited too quickly. He needed time to let it sink in.

While he was at the gym, I took a second pregnancy test, which only confirmed the wonderful news. I called my mother, and together we wept over the phone. By the time Paul got home, I had purchased *What to Expect When You're Expecting* at the mall and read the entire first chapter.

"I took another test," I told him, placing it next to the first one for him to see.

Paul looked at it and then shook his head.

"After all we've been through, it seems too good to be true," he answered, gathering me into his arms. "I just can't believe it."

Miracles, a Country Apart

☙☙☙

For several years, I believed that if I could have gone back in time and saved ourselves from the expense and moral responsibility of those fertility treatments, I would have. The amount of money Paul and I spent trying to get pregnant actually neared six figures. I often wondered if we had been wrong to mess with God's creation process since he obviously and ultimately had the last say, anyway.

There was nothing medically wrong with either of us, except our age. It's normal for a woman's fertility to decrease after the age of 35, and we were already in our late 30s when we met and married.

The fertility process was long and difficult. We started out with oral medication, and when that didn't work, we moved on to intrauterine insemination, or IUI. At each step, it was hard to picture that we'd ever have to go on to the next level. We were hopeful that the current treatment would work. But suddenly, after several IUIs, we found ourselves facing in vitro fertilization (IVF). We desperately wanted a child, so we tried IVF three times. Every time it was unsuccessful, and each time was extremely heartbreaking. It just didn't seem possible for me to have a baby.

"I think we should try donor eggs," my doctor said after our last IVF attempt. "Unfortunately, your eggs are probably too old, Linda. Using a donor would be the next step."

At the time, it made sense to us. At least the baby

would have half of our DNA, and I would still get to carry and deliver the baby. Like the doctor said, if we wanted a family, this was what we would have to do. And I was *desperate* to have a family.

We chose an egg donor of Eastern European descent with brown hair and eyes like me. Using Paul's sperm, another set of embryos was created, and we started the IVF transfer process yet again. Each attempt became a blur of tiresome hormone injections laced with hope, followed by the IVF procedure and crushing disappointment. We tried IVF with donor eggs two times, and in the fall of 2006, with two embryos remaining, I decided I was done. I was burnt out on fertility treatments and ready to look at the obvious next step, adoption, after the holidays were through.

But God had a different plan in store for us. When I realized one day at work that my period was unusually late, I dashed to the nearest drugstore to buy a pregnancy test. I could hardly believe my eyes. The pregnancy caught both of us completely off guard. Family and friends rejoiced with us, as all of them had lived through our agony and supported us in trying to start a family.

In September 2007, we welcomed our beautiful miracle daughter, Anne, and she quickly became the light of our lives.

☙☙☙

Miracles, a Country Apart

I had been raised Catholic, and though I was no longer practicing, I wanted Anne to be baptized in the church. I attended some classes to re-familiarize myself with the faith and was surprised to find myself drawn back to God, gaining a new closeness and revitalized intimacy with him.

As Anne grew and the years went by, it bothered us that we still had two remaining frozen embryos. I had no desire to try another embryo transfer since all other transfers had failed. Paul was worried about issues that may arise if we had two children in the family — one of whom was biologically his, and one of whom was biologically both of ours. It was something that had not occurred to us at the beginning of the process. The entire situation felt extremely complicated, and there seemed to be no real right answer.

Finally, we consulted with our priest. He talked us through the dilemma, and we came to the conclusion that because we believed life begins at conception, the embryos could not be thrown away or donated to science. And if I wasn't willing to go through another embryo transfer again, the only remaining option was to donate them to another couple who could go through the embryo transfer process themselves and, if successful, raise the baby as their own. Our priest blessed the decision.

I began to research online for embryo adoption agencies across the country, but all I found was tons of bureaucracy, legal paperwork and checklists that piled up overwhelmingly on my desk for several months. There had to be an easier way.

Souls on Ice

In talking with a friend at our church one day, I learned about an embryo adoption agency near Seattle. I looked up Embryo Adoption Services of Cedar Park online and called Maria Lancaster the very next day. My conversation with Maria was the exact opposite of anything I had experienced with the other agencies. I was impressed by her warmth and passion, as well as the fact that the process at her agency seemed streamlined and simple. I felt in my heart that we had found our answer.

❧❧❧

It was the spring of 2012. Maria sat on the sofa in our living room, sharing her personal experience and the stories of many others whose lives had been blessed by embryo donation and adoption.

With each positive outcome she shared, Paul and I were more and more convinced that this is what we wanted to do with our remaining frozen embryos. But, for many reasons, we weren't ready for an open adoption. We didn't know how much contact we would want to have at first.

"I believe that God guides this process and leads us in knowing where each embryo should go," Maria said. "And when I look at you and your home and your family, I am reminded of a particular couple on the East Coast. They have a similar church background, and you'll see in their photos that even their home is similar to yours. They are in their 40s, and she is from Spain."

Miracles, a Country Apart

The more she talked, the more passion I could detect in Maria's summation of this couple. She clearly thought they would be a perfect match for our embryos, so she brought us an extensive book that Frank and Paloma had put together describing their lives.

As we flipped through the pages, we were impressed with their world travels and their career choices. They seemed like us in a lot of ways. They were devoted Christians, with Catholic backgrounds. We even loved that Frank could play the organ. Music was always a joy for us. Education, family, healthy living and faith seemed as important to them as it was to us. And Maria was right: Photos of their home showed that our house interiors were eerily similar. They seemed like a really nice couple who really wanted a child.

"They're the ones," I said, closing the book decisively.

Paul nodded his head in agreement. "I actually like that they will be older parents, like we are."

"Oh, they will be so thrilled. I can't wait to tell them!" Maria beamed.

☙☙☙

The process moved rather quickly, and before we knew it, the embryos were sent off to the adopting couple in New England.

I was nervous and concerned for Paloma, this woman I had never even met but for whom I felt such growing affection. After all, we knew the pain of losing embryos.

Souls on Ice

How was this possibly going to be successful for Paloma with only two embryos?

We grieved when we learned that the first transfer had ended in loss. Frank and Paloma chose to put off the second transfer for a few more months, and in the meantime, we prayed. Having been through the torture of failed embryo transfers through this process, we knew almost exactly what they were going through.

In October, Maria called us with the news we had been waiting for.

"Paloma's pregnant! It worked!"

"Oh, my goodness, that's wonderful!" I replied, tears filling my eyes. "I can't wait to tell Paul!"

We were thrilled for Frank and Paloma. How crazy it was that out of all of our embryos and all of our unsuccessful attempts, *the very last one* had made it for her! It was truly a miracle.

Paul and I felt strangely emotional about it, too — even feeling some grief for giving away our flesh and blood. Even though the embryo was from a donor egg and was not biologically mine, it was my sweat, tears and agony. Maybe it wasn't technically related to me, but I thought of it as mine in every other way.

Over the next few months, Paul and I struggled to come to terms with our new reality. We had wanted a semi-open adoption for several reasons, and there was never any regret for giving away our embryos to Frank and Paloma. But there was an underlying curiosity about this life that was growing on the other side of the country

Miracles, a Country Apart

… this miracle person so similar to our own miracle daughter, Anne. Even though we'd never met Frank and Paloma, we thought about them and prayed for them constantly and considered them part of our extended "family."

About a week before Paloma's due date, I found myself weeping all day. I could not stop crying. I had not expected to be so emotional.

Out of desperation, we called Maria. She arrived on our doorstep ready to lavish us with answers and hope.

"What you're feeling is completely normal and natural," she explained gently. "You have essentially given up a child for adoption. But you must remember that this child will bring so much joy to Paloma and Frank, just like Anne has brought to you."

I nodded through my tears, feeling like a blubbering mess.

"This baby is a miracle," she continued, "and God led every single step in this process. He wants this baby to be raised in that specific family for a specific reason."

I knew she was right. I wiped my wet cheeks with a tissue and took a deep breath, trying to stop more tears from coming.

Then, almost as an afterthought, Maria added, "Linda, is there something you want to give them?"

"Yes!" It was suddenly very clear. This is what I had subconsciously been thinking about all along! I ran upstairs to our bedroom and grabbed a picture of Anne as a baby. Out of my dresser drawer, I took a gold baby-sized

Miraculous Medal, which was a precious and meaningful token of my Catholic faith. I believed in my heart that Frank and Paloma should have it for their baby. I prayed that the baby would be safe and would grow to know God as her protector.

I returned to the living room and handed the photo and medal to Maria. "If you could pass these on to them, I would really appreciate it."

"Of course!" Maria agreed.

She then spent the next several hours with Paul and me, explaining the protocol for after the baby's birth. All communication would continue to go through her. She explained what we could expect from the adopting parents and what emotions to continue to expect of ourselves. It was important to understand that they needed space as new parents to establish their own family unit. Over the months of Paloma's pregnancy, Paul and I had realized that we differed in opinion somewhat on the kind of contact we wanted to have between our families. Maria was able to provide information and guidance that put us more on the same page. While we were thrilled that Frank and Paloma had our embryo and would soon have a baby, a relationship beyond that was still unknown, and it was best to let things evolve naturally as time went on.

By the time Maria left — the gifts for Frank and Paloma stowed safely in her purse — Paul and I were much more at peace about the situation. And we could hardly wait for the joyous news of the baby's birth.

Miracles, a Country Apart

❧❧❧

I stood at the mailbox and let out a little squeal of glee when I saw "Embryo Adoption Services of Cedar Park" on the return address of the priority envelope. This was the piece of mail we had been waiting for. I tucked it under my arm to keep it safe from the gentle summer rain.

"Paul!" I called, as I entered the house. "I think we got the birth announcement!"

Maria had called with the good news a few weeks earlier, but we were so excited to finally see a picture of Frank and Paloma's baby girl.

Paul joined me in the kitchen as I tore the envelope open and slid out a lovely pink birth announcement for Isabel Maria. With it was a photograph of a tiny sleeping baby. I gasped.

"Oh, Paul, she looks just like you!" I exclaimed. "How crazy is that?"

"You think so? I think she looks like Anne."

"Yes, she does look like Anne, too. She's simply beautiful."

"She is," Paul agreed.

My heart leapt with the joy I felt for Frank and Paloma and their long-awaited child. I placed the treasured picture of Isabel Maria in my wallet so I could see her often, and I hung the birth announcement in my prayer area where I could continue to thank God for sweet Isabel Maria's life.

❧❧❧

Souls on Ice

At Mass the next Sunday, I sought out our priest. Since he had counseled us and blessed our decision to donate our frozen embryos in the first place, I wanted to share our joy with him.

"Father, the couple who adopted our embryos gave birth! They have a daughter!"

His face broke into a broad grin, and he gave me a huge hug.

"What wonderful news!" he exclaimed. "Praise be to God!"

༄༄༄

A month later, I received another envelope from Maria. This one contained an intimate letter from Paloma herself, thanking me for the gifts we sent her via Maria. The letter went on to explain that they had experienced several close calls during the pregnancy. Each time, she and Frank believed that God had intervened and saved their daughter's life.

"*And you have given me the Miraculous Medal,*" Paloma wrote. "*I cannot think of a more appropriate thing.*"

Isabel Maria's life was a true miracle in every sense of the word.

༄༄༄

Miracles, a Country Apart

"Mommy, I want a little sister or brother." Six-year-old Anne would often say this, and each time I felt my heart catch in my throat. This time, we were walking as a family on a lovely beach off the Northwest coastline.

"I think our family is perfect just the way it is," Paul said. "We have you."

Anne giggled, and Paul and I exchanged knowing glances, our thoughts wandering to the little family somewhere on the other side of the country, raising a biological half-sister. We didn't know what the future held. Maybe they would meet someday.

We put our hope and trust in God, that he would work things out the way he wanted them to be. In a lot of ways, our story was just beginning. We would just have to wait and see how God's plan would unfold. We had certainly learned through our journey to trust God and his perfect plan.

All I knew was that it was a miracle that through the pain of our infertility, God had taken care of us, and then he had taken care of Frank and Paloma, too. The horrible, painful experience had turned into a blessing for two separate families. All those treatments and struggles were used for good by God. That whole time we were doing IVF, we had no idea that those embryos would be a gift for another suffering family.

God had certainly worked all things together for good, replacing our pain with joy. And as Paul and I walked along the beach hand-in-hand, watching *our* miracle daughter dip her feet in the lapping water, we were perfectly at peace knowing that thousands of miles away, on the other coastline, another miracle named Isabel Maria was *exactly* where she was supposed to be.

"And we know that all things work together for good to those who love God, to those who are the called according to his purpose." (Romans 8:28)

Our Gift
The Adoption Story of Frank and Paloma
Written by Joy Steiner Moore

The wind blew in heavy white gusts around our house, circling the tree outside our living room window. I stood at the glass and watched as countless snowflakes swirled aimlessly through the air and came to rest at last in our front yard, creating drifts over the road and against the house across the street.

It was a "nor'easter," as they called it — a powerful New England blizzard strong enough to shut down businesses and schools not only in our quaint coastal village, but throughout the entire region.

"Frank? I think I found something."

At the excitement in my wife's voice, I turned around. Paloma sat on the sofa, her laptop perched on her knees, her dark hair framing her lovely face. Since we were snowed in and homebound, we had spent the last couple of hours researching our family planning options. The problem was that though we had only been married for two years, we were already in our mid-40s, so our possibilities seemed to be running out.

I walked over and stood behind Paloma, leaning over her shoulder to look at the computer screen.

"It's another embryo adoption agency," she explained,

Souls on Ice

her beautiful Spanish accent inflecting each word. "But this one is supported by a church. It looks really good."

"You mean they're not just mailing random embryos out of their kitchen freezer?" I teased. Since learning about embryo adoption just that morning, Paloma and I had come across some very odd agencies. Some were very flippant about the process, promising quick delivery, almost like they were running an "embryo-to-go" operation. One thing we knew for sure: While the idea of embryo adoption was intriguing, it certainly didn't seem like something that should be taken lightly. We needed to know more.

Paloma smiled and glanced at the clock. "I think we should call this organization. They're in Seattle, so they're three hours behind us."

I nodded and took a sip of my coffee.

Usually we were "e-mail people," but the one thing this blizzard had given us was the gift of time. Why should we wait for an answer when we could just call this agency directly?

I dialed the phone number on the Web site and was surprised when our call was answered on the first ring.

"Embryo Adoption Services of Cedar Park, this is Maria."

I introduced my wife and myself and gave Maria the basic rundown of our inability to start a family. Over the next half hour, she listened with great interest and then explained the process of embryo adoption. It turned out that Maria was the founder of the agency. She was

Our Gift

passionate, yet articulate, and we felt like the information she gave us was very clear. Before getting off the phone, Maria prayed with us and asked God to direct us in our endeavor.

When we hung up, I saw a glimmer of hope in Paloma's eyes. How quickly our situation had changed! We both knew that the hand of God was on our lives and that *this* was the avenue we were supposed to pursue.

Is there an embryo frozen somewhere, just for us? Does our son or daughter already exist?

Outside, the snow was still falling heavily. It was one of many blizzards that New England would experience in the winter of 2011, but God used that particular storm to clear away many distractions and lead us down a life-changing path.

෴෴෴

When I met Paloma, we were both living and working in Europe. A native of Spain, she was introduced to me by a mutual friend who brought her to an Advent service at my Anglican church. We hit it off right away. She taught Spanish at the university level, and I was drawn to her intelligence, her loving spirit and her commitment to God. Since she also spoke English, and I spoke some Spanish, we had no trouble communicating.

We married in 2009 and moved to the United States to start our lives together. Since we were in our 40s, we knew there was no time to lose in starting a family. But when we didn't get pregnant right away, we visited a fertility clinic to run the necessary tests.

We were glad when the endocrinologist told us that Paloma's hormone levels were those of a woman 10 years younger than she actually was. She suggested we try intrauterine insemination, or IUI. We did, but it was unsuccessful. The doctor surmised that because of Paloma's age, it was possible that even though her hormones were okay, her eggs were just not of good quality. Further IUI procedures would not be advisable. We discussed the possibility of IVF (in vitro fertilization) but realized that in order for it to work, we would need to use a donor egg with my sperm.

Paloma and I were very discouraged. Even though there's an unspoken pressure on men to have a son or daughter from their own bloodline, I didn't want to leave my wife out of the conception process. When I thought about leafing through a book of pictures of egg donors and choosing a woman who might look like Paloma in hopes that the child would believably look like the two of us, I didn't feel right. It felt impersonal to me. I decided that since Paloma's eggs couldn't be used, I didn't want to be the sole contributor to the process. We would have to go another route.

We turned our attention to traditional adoption. We met with an agency and were told that international adoptions could take up to five years, and that just seemed way too long for us to wait. As far as domestic adoption, we learned it wasn't possible for us to adopt a child under the age of 10. The more we thought about it and prayed about it, we didn't believe that we would have an easy time suddenly handling a child as they entered their teen years. It just wasn't the parenting situation we were looking for.

Life moved on, and we got busy — me with my work and Paloma with her teaching. The dream to become parents and have a family together remained very much alive in both of our hearts. But it wasn't until the blizzard forced our lives to a halt that we found ourselves isolated and available for the first time to really listen to what God was saying. It was then that he introduced a possibility we had never even thought of before. In fact, we hadn't even known it existed.

※ ※ ※

We loved the idea of frozen embryo adoption. The way we saw it, there was no reason to try IVF and create an embryo with my DNA when there were already thousands of babies just waiting to be born. It made perfect sense to us as Christians, too, since we believed strongly that life begins at conception and each of these conceived embryos was a life waiting to be lived. It felt like the perfect solution to our infertility problems. A donated embryo would bypass our entire dilemma with Paloma's poor quality of eggs and my lack of desire to use my sperm with a donated egg. The playing field would be leveled, so to speak.

One of the first things we had to do was find a fertility

Souls on Ice

doctor who would agree to help us. Paloma's age was the primary concern, and we had to find a physician who would be willing to treat her with the necessary hormones and then do the actual transfer of the embryo to Paloma's uterus. After speaking with and visiting multiple clinics, we ended up with our original endocrinologist. She was the only one in the city who agreed to do it. She really wanted to see us have a baby.

We began the process of completing the paperwork. It was a lot of work, but Maria at Embryo Adoption Services encouraged us that every bit of it would be worth the trouble when we finally held our baby in our arms.

Maria also asked us to put together a comprehensive book about the two of us. It needed to be detailed and persuasive, so couples with frozen embryos could choose the perfect family for their babies to grow up in.

As we wrote out our story and attached photographs of our wedding, our home, our pets and our travels, I was struck by the irony that the donor family would know much more about where their embryo was going than we would know about where our embryo came from. We prayed that our book would accurately reflect who Paloma and I were as people and the immense love that awaited a future child in our home. We asked God to use our book to guide the right donor family and embryo to us. Then we sent it off to Maria in Seattle and began our wait.

※※※

Our Gift

It was July of 2011, and the Northeast was experiencing an unprecedented heat wave. Of course, this coincided with the home visit from the social worker who flew out from Washington to ensure that we could provide a decent home for a baby.

The temperature was 98 degrees with high humidity the day we welcomed the social worker into our house. Because overly hot weather isn't so common along the New England coastline, not many homes have air conditioning, ours included. We had opened all our windows, attempting to create a cross breeze, but even with high-powered fans placed at crucial points throughout the house, there was no getting around it. It was *hot*.

We sat on the sofas in our front room, drenched in sweat, sipping our ice-cold drinks, hoping with all our hearts that the social worker could overlook the sauna-like conditions and recognize how much love we could give a child.

A few weeks later, we got the call we were waiting for.

"She loved you both!" Maria's voice was ecstatic. "She thought your home was lovely, and she thinks you'll be great parents! You're approved!"

We were so relieved and felt like a heavy burden had been lifted from our shoulders. We just needed to keep praying for the right embryo to come along.

Souls on Ice

"Good news! I found a donor couple who is interested in you!" I could hear Maria's voice, even though it was Paloma who held the phone.

My wife's face glowed with her excitement. She leaned back against the kitchen counter. "That's wonderful!"

"Yes, I will let you know when there's something definite."

"Okay! Thank you!" Paloma's eyes fairly danced with happiness. My heart soared.

We're going to have a baby!

❧❧❧

The next phone call from Maria wasn't so joyful. The donor couple had decided at the last minute to choose a different adopting couple.

"Is it because of our age?" I asked her, trying not to sound bitter.

"It could be." Maria wasn't one to mince words. "But we have to remember God has a plan. He has a better plan than what we thought we had."

Over the next few weeks and months, my wife and I took many walks on the beach near our home. The fresh ocean air invigorated our thought processes, just as the vast sea itself reminded us that God was so much bigger and more capable than we could fully understand. It was very difficult to wait when we felt like each second that ticked by was another second of wasted time. We weren't getting any younger. And yet, we knew that if God had led our steps this far, he certainly would continue guiding the entire process.

At last, after three months, in the spring of 2012, Maria notified us that we had been chosen. The donor couple was from the West Coast and had two embryos to give. The embryos were remaining from their own IVF attempts using an egg donor. We were absolutely overjoyed!

When the embryos arrived, Paloma began the daily hormone injections to prepare her body for the transfer. We were so hopeful and excited. We transferred one embryo, and afterward, the doctor told her to go home and take it easy for a few days. Once again, an unusual New England heat wave seemed to weigh ominously on the situation, and my wife found herself lying on a couch for two 100-degree days in June, fans aimed directly at her face.

But within 10 days, Paloma experienced some light bleeding. The embryo had passed through her body like a very early miscarriage. She wasn't pregnant. I asked the doctor if the heat had played any part in the loss, and she assured us that it had nothing to do with it. It just wasn't meant to be.

The disappointment a couple feels during the pain of infertility is like none other. We were filled with such hope and excitement, followed by such a quick letdown. And we were suddenly worried because we realized we only had one more embryo left — just one more shot at this.

We were planning a trip to Spain for later in the

Souls on Ice

summer and decided to wait until we were back home before starting the long, grueling process of hormone injections once again. It would be our last chance at starting a family.

❧❧❧

Paloma lay quietly on the examination bed, while the endocrinologist prepared the ultrasound equipment. Our eyes met, and I knew what my wife was thinking. She was nervous. Good news was almost too much to hope for.

It was October, and the second embryo transfer was complete. Four months had passed since our first try, and we had visited Paloma's family in Spain. Paloma endured more doctor's appointments and hormone injections and submitted to the requisite bed rest after the embryo transfer took place a little more than a week earlier. Four months had whittled its way down to mere minutes, and now we would know the results. My stomach was in knots.

I squeezed Paloma's hand as the ultrasound got underway.

The doctor moved the wand around and stared stoically at the screen. Then, suddenly, her face broke into a broad smile.

"Look at that! There's a heartbeat!"

My eyes widened, and Paloma and I looked at each other, dumbfounded.

"You're sure?" I asked.

The doctor nodded enthusiastically, the smile never

Our Gift

leaving her face. "You have a baby! Congratulations!"

I leaned over and kissed my wife. There were not words to express our gratitude to God. What a *tremendous gift* this baby would be.

❧❧❧

The late November morning was still very dark as we headed into work. We took our usual route along the shoreline, and we watched as the horizon over the ocean ever so slowly welcomed the light of another day. It was only 6:30 a.m., but rush-hour traffic was already picking up.

Crash!

The vehicle behind us hadn't braked in time, and it slammed violently into the rear of our car.

Paloma screamed.

"The baby! The baby!" She placed her hands protectively on her stomach. She was only nine weeks pregnant.

My heart raced as I quickly helped my wife unbuckle her seatbelt and get out of the car. She seemed unhurt on the outside, but we needed to get to the doctor's office as soon as possible. I knew a miscarriage would be crushing to both of us. We began to pray.

Oh, God, please. Please preserve this child.

One look at our six-month-old vehicle told me it was totaled. It was actually quite impressive that we were able to walk away from it without visible injuries.

Souls on Ice

We rushed to our doctor's office where the midwife immediately did an ultrasound. "I hear the heartbeat!" she said.

Paloma and I exchanged glances and breathed a sigh of relief.

"And if you can hear the baby this strong at nine weeks," the midwife continued, "then you have a 90 percent likelihood of having a strong pregnancy and healthy baby."

Tears of joy streamed down Paloma's cheeks.
Thank you, Lord!

❧❧❧

A couple of weeks after the car accident, my wife had a routine prenatal exam with her obstetrician, who discovered a polyp.

"It's not a problem. It's low enough down that I think I can remove the polyp pretty easily," the young doctor said with confidence.

But her associate didn't agree. "It's too risky. Just leave it there until the end of the pregnancy."

The younger doctor was so insistent and confident that we were finally persuaded to have her remove the polyp. Of course, we had to sign a mountain of paperwork absolving her from any responsibility should we lose the baby as a result of the procedure. But the doctor assured us repeatedly that there was no real risk.

A few days after the procedure, Paloma was at home

Our Gift

packing for our Christmas vacation to Europe when she started to bleed profusely. She was hemorrhaging. I rushed her to the emergency room.

"It looks like it's likely that a miscarriage is beginning and well underway," the ER doctor said grimly. "I'm very sorry."

Paloma covered her face with her hands and stifled a sob. I gently put my arm around her and held her.

"We have this trip planned for Christmas," Paloma said at last. "Is there a way I can still get on the plane tomorrow?"

The doctor raised an eyebrow in surprise. But I knew that my wife had been looking forward to being with her family for the holidays, and she would need their love and support even more so during a miscarriage.

"Well, you may have a miscarriage while you are on the plane," the doctor answered. She shook her head as if to say she would not advise it and offered to pray for Paloma.

We drove home in silence. There was nothing to say. It was a situation completely out of our control. When we pulled up in our driveway, Paloma climbed out of the car and walked slowly up the moonlit path to our house. She sat down in the living room, which was illuminated only by the tiny lights of the Christmas tree.

"Frank?"

"Yes, sweetheart?"

"We need to pray. God can stop this miscarriage. He has already protected this baby through being a frozen

Souls on Ice

embryo for several years. He has already protected the baby through the car accident. We know he has a plan for this child."

I agreed completely.

So we spent a very tense night praying hard together, thanking God for the child in Paloma's womb. We prayed for her healing, for the bleeding to stop. We prayed for God's hand to be present and evident in every part of Paloma's and the baby's bodies.

When morning came, the bleeding had stopped. My wife called the obstetrician who was still on duty from the night before and explained the situation.

"Well, if the bleeding has stopped, you're fine," the doctor said. "A miscarriage would have gone on for much longer. Go get on the plane!"

Paloma and I believed completely that the Lord had intervened and halted the miscarriage. It was a true miracle. The ER doctor had said that a miscarriage was imminent, but we knew that God really wanted this baby to live. He really wanted us to have this child.

Our faith strengthened by our answered prayer, we hopped on the plane and had a wonderful Christmas in Spain. Paloma had a very normal and healthy remainder of her pregnancy, and we looked forward to meeting our baby in June.

☙☙☙

Our Gift

Our daughter, Isabel Maria, was born on June 25, 2013, absolutely perfect in every way. It was the happiest moment of our lives.

Our friends and family shared our joy. Paloma's parents came from Spain and stayed for a month to help us out, which we appreciated, having had no real experience with babies ourselves.

We had chosen a name that we believed would fit well in both our cultures and languages. We planned to raise Isabel bilingually.

I called Maria at the agency and gave her the good news about Isabel Maria's birth.

"I like the middle name!" she joked in response. I could hear the smile in her voice. She was so happy to hear that everything had gone so well. I thanked her again and again for everything she had done to make our dream of having a family come true.

As the months went by, and my wife and I bonded with our baby girl, I began contemplating the meaning of fatherhood. I thought about the donor family, living their lives across the country, somewhere on the West Coast. We knew little more about them than their first names, but I hoped that Paul and Linda knew how grateful we were for the tiny embryos they had given up — that they had released into our care. I was confident that God had directed their actions and that *his* hand was in the entire process.

I worried somewhat about my age. When I did the math and realized how old we would be when Isabel graduated from college, I wanted to laugh. But I knew that even younger couples didn't know the future when they planned their families. God had his hand on Isabel's life and would keep her from harm.

In the end, I understood that God had created our bodies to have children. Whether it happened naturally from our own genetics or in a different way, such as adoption or embryo adoption, each child belonged to God and was on loan from him. Paloma was merely the medium God used to bring Isabel into the world. The child was not ours, and she wasn't Paul and Linda's. She was God's. And as her parents, it was our mission and responsibility to introduce her to God as her real father. God obviously wanted Isabel on the earth. Now it was our duty to instill in her the values and Christian beliefs that would set her on the path of the unique and special plan God had for her life.

༄༄༄

I watched as Paloma carefully placed Isabel into her stroller and fastened the safety belts.

"We're going for a walk, Isabel," she crooned in Spanish. "You like our walks to the beach, don't you?"

Isabel kicked her legs in response and offered a sweet toothless grin. My heart melted for the thousandth time. How I *loved* being a dad.

It was a warm evening, and I knew that when we got home, we would be glad for the bedroom air conditioning

Our Gift

units I had installed shortly before Isabel was born. We would sleep soundly that night.

By late summer, the long evening walks had become a daily routine for us. We'd stroll lazily through our neighborhood, enjoying the sights, sounds and smells of families grilling, playing and enjoying each other's company. When we got to the beach, we'd breathe deeply of the air and listen to the relaxing sound of the lapping water. When we'd had our fill, we would return home the same way we'd come, our path guided by streetlights and the glowing windows of the homes we passed.

Neighbors would occasionally stop us and admire our sleeping infant, offering their congratulations and commenting on how much our baby resembled both of us. Paloma and I would just smile politely and thank them, fascinated ourselves by God's handiwork and knowing we had nothing to do with our daughter's beauty.

We enjoy being together, our little family. I had to go all the way to Europe to find Paloma. Isabel had been shipped to us frozen from the other side of the United States, where she had existed before Paloma and I even met. I'm convinced that our daughter's life is special — on loan to us, entrusted to us by her creator. Together, the three of us make a real family — one handpicked and designed by God himself.

> "Before I formed you in the womb I knew you,
> before you were born I set you apart." (Jeremiah 1:5 NIV)

Souls on Ice

Isabel Maria

The Life Spark
The Adoption Story of Christine and Anthony
Written by Marty Minchin

We called it our "Hail Mary." Our last chance prayer.

I was 42 years old, and all of our attempts at pregnancy had failed, including one that ended in a dreadful miscarriage at eight weeks. This second try at in vitro fertilization had produced three viable embryos, and one had implanted. This was to be our last go at having a baby — this physically and emotionally trying process was wearing us out.

The doctors at our high-risk clinic in Vancouver, where I had been a patient for years through our attempts at pregnancy, were thrilled that I was pregnant. The sobering charts and graphs they'd pulled out showed that the chances of me conceiving were low, but here I was at eight weeks with a fetus developing right on track.

Every day, I thanked God for the growing baby inside me. I talked to the baby, telling him or her how happy Anthony and I were that he or she was coming into our lives. How much he or she was loved and wanted.

I relaxed on the examination table as the ultrasound image flashed onto the screen.

The night before, I'd had a bad cough, and a particularly bad one had caused a pain in my stomach. I

Souls on Ice

was sensitive to every tiny change in my body and environment, wondering if it would affect the baby.

The room grew quiet as the doctor moved the ultrasound wand around my uterus. We had seen these images so many times in the past that our eyes knew to search immediately for the flickering heartbeat.

Out of the corner of my eye, I saw Anthony slump over. I squinted at the screen, searching for the glimmer of light that would indicate life. The doctor carried on taking notes and measurements, refusing to acknowledge what we all knew we were seeing.

There was no heartbeat. The baby had died and with it our fervent hopes that we would one day be parents.

☙☙☙

Anthony and I first met in the mid-1990s. We worked for the same firm in Vancouver, and we'd occasionally end up at lunch together with mutual friends from the office. We were not particularly drawn to each other. I was going through a very disappointing divorce. Anthony was raised in South Africa by Chinese parents, and his outlook on life didn't jibe with mine. In Canada, many people are brought up with a socialist mindset of helping others. Anthony seemed more interested in earning money. Our outlooks on life had little in common at the time.

I eventually left the firm I was working for and finalized my divorce. I spent the next few years as a single woman, and I gradually began to make peace with the idea

The Life Spark

that I wouldn't have children. Plenty of my friends were single, too, and we settled into a fun, active lifestyle with a group of people in like situations. We went to parties, movies and out to dinner.

A group plan to see a movie fell apart one weekend night. Everyone canceled except me and Anthony, who also had divorced and had joined my crowd of singles. We decided to go to the movie, anyway, and I found myself looking forward to hanging out with him. He was funny, and I could see that over the years his values and overall attitude had changed.

Without the chatter of a group, our impromptu movie date gave Anthony and me a chance to really get to know each other. I liked his sense of stability and his plans for the future. Much of his extended Chinese family had immigrated to Vancouver to escape political and social unrest in South Africa, and I liked that he cared about them so much. Plus, he was so funny. I was glad to spend time with someone who could appreciate the lighter side of life.

Anthony was seeing me differently as well. He liked that I would stop on the street and help someone. He saw me as caring and giving. Our friendly night at the movies quickly turned into a romantic relationship, and in 2005, we decided to commit to each other. Our relationship was built on a solid foundation of friendship, and we found it easy to communicate. When we were apart, we missed each other. When we traveled together, we thoroughly enjoyed each other's company. As accountants, we

Souls on Ice

understood that sometimes our jobs required working long hours. Because we'd had prior failures in our relationships, we'd learned that little things don't really matter. If it was a beautiful day outside, we decided spending time with each other was more important than chores.

On one of our frequent trips, Anthony surprised me when he broached a new topic of conversation.

"It's suddenly really important for me to get married, settle down and have a child," he said.

I sat up straight at this news.

"I need time to think about that."

I had been pregnant years before. In my first marriage, a miscarriage had landed me in the hospital with horrific hemorrhaging. But the more I thought about Anthony's realization, the more I thought, why not? We loved each other. We had a lot to offer a child. I'd gotten pregnant before, so I knew I could.

We knew that Anthony had a bit of a malefactor. When he was young, doctors treated an eye problem with powerful steroids that had damaged his sperm production. Under a microscope, you could see the tailless sperm swimming in circles — like men, I joked, who refused to ask for directions. Still, doctors said there were enough healthy ones that I could get pregnant. In July 2008, a pregnancy test proved them right.

The test solidified the discussions Anthony and I had been having about our relationship. Our serious questions about our future together and our suitability were easily

The Life Spark

answered. We wanted to be together and have a family. We had together been developing a faith in God. Anthony had been baptized in the Catholic church as a child, but my family had left the church years ago after my parents had bitterly divorced. The church had never been a place of comfort for me, but Anthony began to strongly feel that he wanted to be part of a church and part of God's plan again.

I began to wonder myself whether getting to know God truly could impact my life, so I enrolled in confirmation class and learned about my faith. Soon I became a confirmed Catholic as well.

The baby didn't live to the nine-week mark. We learned afterward it was a girl, and she had Trisomy 15, a significant chromosomal disorder that most fetuses will die from. While Anthony and I mourned the loss of this little one, the chromosomal disorder explained the baby's death, and almost any woman carrying a baby with Trisomy 15 would have miscarried. We took the blow, knowing that God wanted us to remember what was most important in life. We knew we needed more of God in our lives.

By January, I was pregnant again. The fantastic news thrilled us, but my joy was tempered by my history. Doctors sent us to the high-risk clinic at the local hospital, where I visited weekly for blood tests and ultrasounds. The joy and emotion of pregnancy were being squelched by statistics and numbers as doctors tracked the minute details of my growing baby. The days became long and anxiety-ridden, and I thought about my pregnancy every minute.

This baby's heart stopped between six and seven weeks. Doctors suspected another chromosomal issue, but they assured us we were simply victims of really bad luck.

I was 40 years old, and my odds of a successful pregnancy were dropping, but we decided to continue on. *We'll get lucky,* I assured myself. *We'll have a baby.*

❧❧❧

For many women, pregnancy comes easily. For me, it became an exact, exhausting science.

I filled calendar books with daily records of my basal body temperature, which can indicate when a woman's body ovulates. The spontaneous act of love that was so central to our intimacy became a necessary act on certain days of the month when pregnancy chances were optimal. And behind all of it hung the specter of grief from my previous failures.

All around me, however, the world seemed filled with babies. Friends who weren't even trying got pregnant. Other friends were conceiving their second or third child. Strangers asked whether we were planning to have kids. As each month passed, my desperation grew as everyone around us had children. We were being left behind.

After more than a year of failed attempts, it was time for outside intervention.

We first turned to medicine. I struggled with the idea

The Life Spark

of utilizing medical assistance in pregnancy, wondering if it was giving too much scientific weight to the creation of life. But after significant soul searching, I grew to realize that God provides the life spark, no matter the method of conception. God decides whether life will happen, not science. God is just as involved in medical intervention as he is in unassisted pregnancy.

The medical clinic waiting room became a weekly routine. I'd sit there half-smiling at the other women, checking my watch, wondering which nurse would take blood that day. Sometimes a woman would come in with a child or a huge pregnant belly, and I'd hold my jealousy in check by reminding myself that I was at the clinic to get myself into the same situation.

All of our attempts to control our bodies were only showing us how little control we had. No matter how much work we put into this process, we had no bearing on the outcome.

Anthony and I did not question our commitment to each other, but we decided to honor God and be formally married. *Maybe he will bless us with a baby,* I thought. We were planning a trip to South Africa to attend a cousin's wedding, and my dad was ill, so we decided to get married right away while he was still with us. Our first wedding was an intimate one, with just close family present. We had a larger church wedding six months later that fulfilled our dreams of our wedding day. We felt like the right ordering of our relationship was how God was leading us, and our faith became more central to our lives.

Souls on Ice

The legal status of our relationship, however, didn't seem to ease our infertility issues. We began talking about other options, including all kinds of adoption. Traditional avenues of adoption were backlogged for years, and we were either too old or not married long enough for the adoption standards for many countries. We could put our name on a list for domestic adoption, but chances were we never would get chosen. Some countries had closed their doors to adoption, and to adopt from China we had to present documents proving Anthony's Chinese heritage. Those papers had long been lost in the small villages of his grandparents. If the door to adoption had even opened an inch, we felt like it loudly shut in our faces.

Our remaining choice was in vitro fertilization, with all of its shots, drugs and medical interventions. With time running out, though, we decided to give it a chance. I was 42, and despite my meticulous adherence to the pre-IVF regimen, my ovaries weren't producing like they should. The ovaries of a healthy woman in her mid-20s would produce so many follicles they would look like a cluster of grapes under a microscope. On our first IVF attempt, I produced only three follicles, which release mature eggs. Doctors said there was less than a 1 percent chance of fertilization with so few, so we opted for IUIs instead. Our attempts were unsuccessful.

In desperation, we threw up our "Hail Mary," our second and last IVF attempt. We did not know what else to do. We had run out of options, or so we thought.

The Life Spark

❧❧❧

In the background, however, a hope was flickering like a candle in a far-off window. In the midst of our IVF attempts, a friend I hadn't spoken with in six months called me out of the blue.

"Do you remember me?" she asked. I did — she was a deeply religious Catholic, and I was always glad to hear from her.

"I got this information from a friend, and as soon as I read it, your face came right to my mind. This might be just right for you. Maybe God put you on my mind."

Because she had such a strong connection with God, I took what she said seriously. She was adamant that I get in touch with an agency in the United States that connected couples dealing with infertility to couples who had stored embryos left over from IVF. I had already stumbled across this information searching in Google a few months before, but I had never followed up. I contacted the agency, but they didn't have a lot of information for mixed-race couples. I also called Maria Lancaster at Embryo Adoption Services of Cedar Park. We liked that her agency was just across the border in Washington. Maria always returned my calls. She knew where Canada and Vancouver were, and her agency was a Christian ministry. The idea of embryo adoption sounded hopeful, but we wanted to give our own genetics one last try.

After my miscarriage following my IVF pregnancy, testing showed the baby suffered from another devastating chromosomal disorder. I suffered an inner infection afterward, which meant more trips to the doctor.

On one particularly difficult day, I found myself sitting in an examination room plastered with pictures of smiling babies. I'd just been moved from the waiting room, which had a parade of beautiful women with big bellies. I saw the sick humor in this unintentional situation, but I couldn't look at those cherubic little faces without being sharply reminded of what I'd lost.

"This is a lovely room," I told the nurse when she finally came to check on me. "But it's torturous for me."

"Oh, I'm so sorry!" Her face reddened when she realized what hung on the walls.

"Do you have an office I can sit in instead?"

She mercifully moved me to a doctor's desk chair, but it did little to ease the chasm inside me that was filled with pain and sadness. I went on to see a grief counselor, who helped me mourn the loss of the genetic baby we'd never have. I often cried, sometimes sitting in the car as I watched people with children walk by. A month after my miscarriage, I put my head down and wept during Mass when the priest asked all of the mothers to stand for a special blessing.

Why, God? I'd ask. *Why don't you give us this miracle?*

I told a priest I felt like we were being punished.

"God is not a punishing God," he replied. "He can't change what's wrong. He can be there for you and offer comfort."

The Life Spark

I suppose that's true, but it still feels really mean.

After six months of licking our wounds, Maria called us unexpectedly. Like a well-greased wheel, the embryo adoption process easily started up again.

During our required home study, talking with the social worker proved therapeutic. It felt good to discuss our plans for schooling and discipline for our child. We talked to her about how our family would operate. Our eyes were looking toward the future again, rather than staring at the present. We felt like God was telling us that our genetics may not work, but he had a better plan for our family.

☙☙☙

As we waited several months for the results of our home study and criminal background checks, I continued to find comfort and support in online IVF forums. I had communicated online with forum members for years — some had two or three babies. Members came from all over the world, and it was comforting to know that people were praying for us around the globe.

During this period, Anthony and I had slipped back into our no-kids lifestyle. We had resumed traveling, golfing and snowboarding in Whistler. "Maybe," Anthony would say, "we'll be okay without kids. We'll retire early and travel the world."

I wasn't sure if he really meant that.

During a group chat on one of the boards, a woman

joined in who had twins through IVF and had embryos remaining that she wanted to donate to another family. I e-mailed her separately, telling her we'd be interested in adopting them.

We're a mixed-race couple, I wrote, *and if that's not what your plan is for your family, we totally understand.*

Then we have an interesting connection, she responded. *We are Caucasian and Chinese as well.*

This couple had worked with a clinic in the United States, and after the twins, they had decided they weren't able to care for more children. They had five frozen embryos, but they had to wait six months after their IVF before donating them.

When Maria called wanting to match us with another Chinese/Caucasian mixed-race donor couple, I politely declined because we were committed to the couple I had met in the chat forum. It didn't seem fair to suddenly back out.

Within a week, everything fell apart. I received an e-mail from the donor couple, and the wife said they were having marital issues, were dealing with new twins and felt they couldn't proceed with the embryo adoption. It was too big of a decision, they said. They needed to sort their lives out first.

"Anthony," I said that night as I read the e-mail from the other donor couple Maria had been talking about. "Quick, gut reaction. Read this e-mail from the donor couple we've been waiting for. How do you feel?"

He didn't have to say anything. I walked around to

face him where he sat on the couch. There were tears in his eyes.

We were not done.

֍֍֍

I called Maria the next morning, and she broke the news that she had just matched the Chinese multi-racial embryo with someone else.

God, I cried out. *What do you intend for us? We're getting strong mixed messages.*

Two days later, Maria called back. The match did not work out with the first family. The donors wanted a similarly mixed-race couple that would be willing to consider an open adoption. "That couple could be us!" I told Anthony.

The donating couple had three healthy embryos in a clinic in the United States, just on the other side of the Canadian border in Bellingham, Washington, a short ride from where we lived. The pictures of their own smiling little boy were a giant ray of hope to us. Our emotions were ragged after the rollercoaster we had been on for so many years. Hope filled our hearts, and we prayed.

We went into scrapbooking overdrive, sorting through almost 5,000 pictures and compiling the story of our lives to present to the donor couple. We stayed up until 2 a.m. three nights in a row assembling pictures and text on Shutterfly to create a bound book. Hopefully the donors would choose us to adopt their embryos.

Souls on Ice

Matches have to be mutual, and we knew immediately that we liked this couple. They wanted an open adoption, like we did. We loved the pictures they sent of their beautiful son, who would potentially be our child's brother. They looked down to earth. They were open to our families visiting each other. We loved the idea of our child having two families.

We were jubilant when the couple accepted us as a match and humbled that this lovely couple chose us to receive their embryos. What a beautiful gift.

The couple had three embryos to donate, and we took them all. By late August, I had taken the medical steps necessary to prepare my body for the embryo transfer. One of the three embryos did not survive the thaw, so the two remaining were transferred into me. Doctors told us that the embryos were healthy.

We waited 12 days to see if anything had happened. We prayed every morning and every night for the embryos.

In September, we received a positive pregnancy test and re-enrolled in the high-risk clinic. My first ultrasound showed one baby with a heartbeat at six weeks and one day. We grieved for the loss of one baby and rejoiced in the new life of another.

~~~

Soon after that joyous first ultrasound, I stood up at a Wednesday night church gathering and felt a big rush of blood. Terrified that I was losing the baby, we rushed to the emergency room. Doctors said my cervix was closed, but to be safe, they scheduled another ultrasound for Friday, the earliest appointment available.

Anthony had scheduled a business trip and golf tournament to Phoenix, leaving Thursday. Worry was etched on his face, but I encouraged him to go. He stayed up all night Wednesday and Thursday praying, and his golf score on the first few holes Friday morning reflected his state of mind.

My friend Liz accompanied me to the ultrasound, taking Anthony's place next to me. As the doctor moved the wand around, I peered at the screen looking for a sign of life.

A big round spot flashed into view. *There should be a baby in there.* I squeezed the tissue in my hand. *Please, no.*

The doctor knew what she was doing. With a turn of her hand, the wand offered another view of my uterus. As it flashed around, I spotted it. A little round egg in the yolk sac. Inside, there was what looked like a fruit fly. Then, the flicker of a heartbeat that looked like a tiny butterfly beating its wings.

"The baby is still there!"

Relief rolled over me, and I cried, "Liz, there's a heartbeat!"

I pulled out my cell phone and texted Anthony. *Still a baby. It's still a go.* On the golf course, he broke down in tears.

Souls on Ice

☙☙☙

The road of infertility is long and nothing is ever sure, but we press on, hoping to God for our miracle child. Knowing there was nothing else we could do, we decided to take a month-long trip to Europe. Nothing could be done to prevent another miscarriage. The time together and relaxation would do us both a lot of good.

For the first time, we left behind the medical monitoring that defined my earlier pregnancies. Stripped of science and technology, we had no one but God with us for four weeks. We prayed in every church in Europe on our trip, that God would protect the growing baby inside me. When we arrived home, we had an ultrasound. We watched our little one — alive, healthy, waving and wiggling!

God's plan for us is greater than we could ask or imagine. We trust him to guide us through the uncertainty. We trust that he sees and knows our precious frozen embryo — the little life spark growing inside me.

It's going to be a faith journey.

But God, the creator of life, is in control.

"'For I know the plans I have for you,' declares the Lord, 'plans to prosper you and not to harm you, plans to give you hope and a future.'" (Jeremiah 29:11)

Conclusion

Miracles do happen.

Sometimes we stumble around, suffering and struggling, before we are able to let go of *our* plan and allow God to reveal his perfect plan *for us*. His miracle. At least, that's what happened for Jeff and me in our desire to become parents together.

For us, the key was not to give up, but to surrender. They are two very different things. We never gave up our dream. We never gave up trying. We never gave up looking for answers. But we had to surrender the details. We had to surrender to God's timing. We had to surrender *control.*

It's easy to say and very, very hard to do.

Surrendering means being willing to see something differently — to see it from God's point of view and provision. It is a practice I learned to cultivate and, ultimately, to cherish.

That does not mean I do it perfectly. Not at all. But, somehow, I have learned to let go and pray: "God, I don't even know where to start. Help me to find you. Reveal yourself to me that I might know you. I am sincerely seeking you."

I'll be honest. Those feelings of despair, disappointment and brokenness, those didn't heal immediately. In those moments of grief, I've found it helps to pray: "God, I do know you are with me. Someday this will all make sense. Please, show me your ways, God, so that I may overcome this difficulty."

All I can tell you is, although waiting and trusting and trying is not always comfortable, the rewards are great. We saw our daughter in our mind's eye before we knew her. Our little miracle baby. Our princess. She is the love of our lives.

We've learned that when we order our thoughts and actions to be consistent with the heart of God, that's when we start to see the miracles all around us. As Jeff and I know it is right to show great care and concern to the fragile and frail, we also believe it is right to cherish life in *all* forms, including embryos that need a family.

Nothing could be more vulnerable than a frozen embryo — unseen, unheard, silently waiting.

Maybe you are feeling like embryo adoption might be your path. Maybe you have embryos you feel called to donate to another family. In either case, we would be glad to talk with you and explain your options.

I truly believe God will never abandon a sincere heart. He has a plan for your family, and I have full confidence that the beginning of *your* miracle can start today.

God bless you, your family and the dreams that you desire.

Conclusion

Maria D. Lancaster
Co-Founder & Executive Director
Embryo Adoption Services of Cedar Park
22525 SE 64th Place, Suite 253
Issaquah, WA 98027
888-959-7712
www.AdoptEmbryos.org
www.DonateEmbryos.org
Maria@adoptembryos.org

What Other Families Are Saying...

My husband and I have always wanted children in our family. After trying to conceive for several years on our own, along with several failed IVF cycles, we started looking into embryo adoption. After making several phone calls around the country to several embryo adoption agencies, we were certain we wanted to work with Maria at Embryo Adoption Services of Cedar Park. Maria has been wonderful to work with, gave us hope and was an answer to our prayers! We were matched with a wonderful donating family and now have a beautiful little boy. We wanted to grow our family and worked with Maria again for another matching family. Maria found us another wonderful match, and we are now expecting our second blessing, another boy! Children are a blessing, and we are thrilled to have discovered Embryo Adoption Services of Cedar Park. We are so grateful to the families who have donated their embryos to us. This wonderful gift of life is truly amazing! We are so blessed!!

Melissa and Nic, Illinois

Upon learning that infertility would keep us from having a biological child, we decided to adopt a baby through the foster care system. After having Baby R in our home for 16 months, she was reunified with her birthmother. We were at a bookstore purchasing books on "grief and loss" when we noticed a stack of newspapers with a front-page article regarding embryo adoption. We had never heard of this before, but surely God knew all along which path we were to take. It turns out that the embryos we adopted were conceived in 2008, the same year that Baby R was conceived! Our "forever" child was waiting for us all along! We are blessed with our son, Jordan, and now want to tell the world about embryo adoption!

Linda and Mark, Seattle, Washington

After waiting, hoping and praying for so long that God would answer our prayers, we were able to have an IVF done. What we didn't know was that we would have several embryos remaining from the procedure. I am so thankful that we were able to release them for adoption, to give another couple the chance to have children and to give our embryos a chance at life! Thanks to the Embryo Adoption Services of Cedar Park.

Mindy and Tommy, Arizona

After trying to conceive for a few years without success and finding out we were dealing with numerous fertility problems, we decided to pursue embryo adoption. I (Laura) was familiar with embryo adoption for years, before we were even married, and always felt that if I couldn't have children that I would be interested in this

What Other Families Are Saying...

option. The opportunity to give birth to our adopted baby and bond from the moment of seeing a positive pregnancy test was exciting to us. We were matched within a short amount of time after submitting our profile and welcomed our miracle, William, in 2011. We will forever be grateful to the donating family who made it possible for us to be called "Daddy" and "Mommy."

Matt and Laura, New Mexico

While going through the process of IVF, we never really thought about extra embryos. We were focused on getting a baby. After our daughter was born and our family complete, we then had the decision of what to do with those embryos. After they spent three years in storage, there were so many signs leading us to Cedar Park and donating our embryos for adoption. As Christians, we believe in life at conception, so this was a perfect option for us. We knew our embryos deserved a chance at life. And having struggled with infertility ourselves, we know what it feels like to want a child so badly. We were very happy to be involved in choosing the adoptive family. We are thrilled to know a child has been born to the adoptive parents.

Corey and Kristie, Seattle, Washington

We had never heard of embryo adoption before our infertility doctor mentioned it. However, we knew very quickly it was the right choice for us. We were matched with a donor family who we had a lot in common with and were blessed enough to get pregnant on the first implantation. Now we have the joy of holding the most precious and amazing 4-month-old daughter. We could not be more grateful to our donor family who allowed us to have this chance. It may not have been the way we originally pictured building a family, but looking back, we wouldn't change one single thing. Every tear and moment of sadness led us to our miracle baby and more happiness than we knew was possible. There's not a doubt in our minds that this was God's plan for our life, and we are truly blessed.

Jason and Lori, Earlsboro, Oklahoma

Early in our dating relationship, my wife and I shared our heart's desire with one another, to have children once we were married. This was a key aspect of knowing we were meant for one another, and we looked forward with great anticipation. Month after month passed, becoming a year, and no sign of a pregnancy. We eventually found out that James was clinically infertile. This was a shock and would have seemed like a moment for Dara to reconsider whether James was indeed "the one." She never blinked, but believed, even as the passing months without a baby mounted. We had encountered the idea of embryo adoption before we had any inkling that God would use it to truly turn our mourning into dancing. After walking the heartbreaking road of infertility, the joy of our precious son is indescribable. We know beyond a shadow of a doubt that God intended for him to become a part of

What Other Families Are Saying ...

our family, and we can't wait for the time to bring his sibling out of the deep freeze. We give thanks first to God for the gift of his precious son and our little boy, but also to Embryo Adoption Services of Cedar Park for being his instrument in blessing us so tremendously. We are deeply indebted to our donor family; their gift allowed our dream of a family to become a reality.

James and Dara, Everett, Washington

Having struggled with infertility for years, I understood the heartache associated with unsuccessful repeated treatment attempts. Finally, after a second IVF procedure, my beautiful daughters were born. I was left with a number of frozen embryos, one of which resulted in my sweet son. Still, the question lingered of what to do with the remaining embryos. To me, these embryos were more than a collection of cells. They were life waiting to be born into this world, and so the best choice would be to give them that opportunity. I made the tough decision to donate my remaining embryos to a couple who wanted a child of their own. As a result, many lives have been blessed.

Sarah, Virginia

We were very fortunate to be blessed with a baby girl only nine months after our "late in life" wedding. But when we wanted to expand our little family, we were faced with fertility challenges that resulted in three miscarriages and a lot of expensive treatments. We began to research adoption options and accidentally discovered embryo adoption and EASCP. It was the perfect solution for us. In December 2012, we received the best Christmas gift ever — we were selected by a donor couple to be the recipients and adopting parents of her embryos. We are thrilled to share the news that almost a year later, we are awaiting the arrival of our miracle baby boy. It has been an amazing journey, and we are so blessed to be the chosen parents to this little angel. We can't wait to see the plans that God has for all of us.

Brent and Carol Ann, Renton, Washington

We struggled to have children for many years, then we were told we had a 1 percent chance of ever having children of our own. Today, we have a son conceived naturally (our first miracle), and we are currently expecting our second miracle, a child we adopted through embryo adoption. We are truly grateful for this amazing program. Our children will grow up knowing without a doubt that they are truly special, that they are loved more than anything in the world and that they are exactly the ones that we were meant to raise. Our family is only complete because we have them and because of the opportunity that embryo adoption has given our family.

Gene and Riley, Seattle, Washington

As a married couple, you just assume you will start a family. We see couples all of our lives having children. So why would it be different for us? This is how our journey

What Other Families Are Saying...

began 10 years ago: Our first pregnancy ended after six weeks. The comments were: "Well, most women miscarry their first pregnancy; you can try again." The second pregnancy ended after 14 weeks. Family and friends did not say much. We turned to medical professionals for help. Test after test, drug after drug, we were finally told by a doctor from a well-known organization, "You need to think about what a family is." We decided to move on to another doctor, and we found one who gave us hope. She explained embryo adoption to us, and this was the first time we felt so encouraged. We found Maria Lancaster and Embryo Adoption Services of Cedar Park. We were given hope that our dreams could come true. So today, 10 years later, our dream of becoming parents is on its way. My husband kept showing me how to believe and to have faith. The road was long and hard, but the dream of having a family will soon be our reality, as we are now expecting! This is not how we thought life would go in the beginning, but now we know we have been chosen by God to bring this child into the world, and we are proud to be this baby's parents.

Karen and Scott, Michigan

We always thought we would have a family, until we experienced the devastation of many failed pregnancies. Our desire to be parents remained strong; however, we had to wonder if parenthood was really God's plan for us. We met later in life, and we certainly weren't getting any younger! We wondered if it was just too late for us, yet the

Souls on Ice

thought of not having a family was heartbreaking. We had so much love to give and to share. It seemed like such a waste. But then a friend told us about embryo adoption. It sounded almost too good to be true. For us, we loved the idea of adoption, and we knew that we could love a child as our own, even if he or she was not our genetic child. We also really wanted to experience carrying a child to term. After starting the journey of pregnancy so many times, we wanted the chance to finish it and to bring a child into the world. When we received our match, we were beyond thrilled. As we read about the couple who had donated their embryos to us, we both felt a strong confirmation that God was in this. We knew that he knew every detail about these embryos that were waiting to be born and that he had chosen to use us to offer them a chance at life. They have waited more than 10 years for this chance, and so have we. It feels good to have hope after so much loss. We pray for our little embryos, that God would protect them and that his will would be done in their lives and in ours. We are almost ready to transfer, and we can't wait to see what the future holds. We can't wait to hold our precious child and know that this was the child he always intended for us.

Jen and Lee, Redmond, Washington

We tried for years having our own children and were unsuccessful. When considering adoption, we looked into many avenues. We had already waited so long (seven years) to become parents, the adoption process felt

What Other Families Are Saying...

daunting. With mountains of paperwork, in-depth questionnaires, interviews and tests, it seemed like becoming a family was never going to happen. Not to mention the expense of the various types of adoption. When we heard about embryo adoption from my father-in-law, it was immediately intriguing, but also seemed almost incomprehensible. It was hard to fathom actually carrying someone else's child. After praying for a while and seeking the wisdom of others, it became clear embryo adoption was the right choice for us. It was not an easy choice, as these are uncharted waters, but we knew we could rely on God each step of the way. At times we felt misunderstood, unsure of what to expect and just wanted to be "normal," but now looking at our darling twin boys who love life, we can't imagine it any other way. It is such a privilege to have played a role in rescuing them from the freezer. As soon as they were born, there was an instant connection, and the sting of so many years of doubt and pain was gone. We are so thankful for the work that Embryo Adoption Services of Cedar Park is doing, making life a reality for so many frozen embryos.

Jeff and Leah, Tacoma, Washington

We were pioneers to the extent that the whole concept of embryo adoption was new when we read about it in the newspaper and decided to make inquiries. Four years later, we are the "Aunt" and "Uncle" to a very delightful 3-year-old boy who has wonderful parents and us, a couple of adoring relatives. The friendship with his parents is meaningful. There is a sense of wonder and mystery to how families are made. We were present at the christening of their next children and travel to see this new extended family about three times a year.

Tess Williams, Seattle, Washington

After years of infertility, we adopted our first daughter through a traditional adoption agency. We then heard about embryo adoption and were intrigued. After completing the application process, we were matched with a donor family, and 11 months later, I gave birth to a healthy baby girl who has been a light in our life. We have an open relationship with her genetic family and enjoy spending time with them. We are so thankful to the donor family, and to Cedar Park, for giving us the opportunity to bring our baby girl into the world and have her join our family.

Nat and Karissa, Seattle, Washington

We were married later in life, and after a year of trying to have a child, we consulted a fertility doctor. The doctor recommended IVF. We were successful and were blessed with a beautiful, healthy baby girl. We felt very fortunate to have a healthy daughter, but we were both raised with siblings, and we felt our family was not complete. We began researching types of adoption and felt that embryo adoption was well suited for our family. We found our own donating family on a fertility support group Web site, and since we had already signed up with Embryo

What Other Families Are Saying ...

Adoption Services of Cedar Park, we had EASCP handle all the logistics and legal paperwork. A short while later, we transferred one of the three embryos donated to us and were blessed with a beautiful baby girl on our older daughter's 4th birthday! All it took was a single frozen embryo! We currently have talked to the genetic family and get along very well. We enjoy seeing photos of their children and send photos of our daughter and notes, e-mails and Facebook messages. We cannot express how grateful we are to our daughter's genetic family — they have given us the most amazing, beautiful gift that totally completes our family.

Julia and Rob, Missouri

The journey to become a donor of embryos is a difficult one. It is a journey of faith and finalization. My husband and I tried for about a year to have children. When we realized that we would have to do IVF, it was a shock, but at least we knew that there would be a baby in the end. After two failed attempts, we got pregnant and had a beautiful baby boy. During this time, we had adopted another baby boy. After we had our sons, we knew that we had lots of embryos left and little time to make a decision on what to do with them. It is very expensive to keep them stored, and we were not ready to have another child. I started to do some research about what people's options were in my situation. I knew that I could not discard them. My faith would not allow that. I knew that I wanted to help another woman have the same joy that I had. That's when I found Embryo Adoption Services of Cedar Park and Maria Lancaster. After a lot of praying, my husband and I knew that it was the right decision to help other women. As hard as it is to make the decision not to have your own embryos, it is a gift from God that I can share this miracle with other families. I am truly blessed that there is a place like this and people who have incredible faith that want to help other families bring a miracle into this world.

Tiena S, Washington

When I first started with the IVF process, the thought never occurred to me: *What would I do if I had more embryos than I wanted to use?* Unfortunately, a baby for me was just not in the cards. I had transferred two embryos and failed to get pregnant. My health took a turn for the worse, and I was faced with much uncertainty. From the moment I found out how many embryos I had, I loved each and every one of them. It was the start of life, and it was a miracle. Because I had longed for a child of my own so badly and went through the tireless and painstaking process of IVF, I knew instantly that just "throwing away" my embryos would never be an option. I did further research and talked to my doctor, who suggested to me that I could place them with their clinic so an anonymous couple could receive the embryos. This just didn't feel right to me. I would never know what would become of them, and that really bothered me. I didn't think there was any other options. I didn't know that

What Other Families Are Saying ...

embryos could be placed for adoption. One day, I went browsing on the Internet, and I came across Embryo Adoption Services of Cedar Park. I looked further into it and found out I could place my embryos for adoption in a safe and comfortable environment. I talked with Maria a few times. And my first time talking with her, it felt right. I could pick the family, and it was even up to me what kind of adoption — open, semi-open or closed. It wasn't easy, needless to say, to give my embryos up for adoption, but when I look back at my own experiences and my desire to have a child, I know there are many other couples out there facing the same situation, wanting to have a child of their own. I truly feel that God had blessed me with this gift, and I wanted to give that gift in return to another family that had hoped and prayed the same way I did. My adoptee family has their first son on the way, and there isn't a day that goes by that I am not grateful to them.

Melanie, Nevada

Embryo adoption has been an evidence of God's grace in our lives. Through five years of polycystic ovarian syndrome related infertility, we tried many hormonal treatments and were encouraged by our doctors to try IVF. Wanting to steward our money well and care for children in as ethical a manner as possible, we chose not to attempt any IVF cycles. As we began a traditional domestic adoption process, we were introduced to Embryo Adoption Services of Cedar Park. We were able to move quickly through the application, home study and matching process. There were challenges along the way as we faced a type-1 diabetic pregnancy, pre-eclampsia and loss of life as some of the embryos did not survive transfer or implant, but through it all, God has blessed us and cared for us, growing our little family in his time and provision. Our hearts are healed by him, both in our grief and happiness. We have a beautiful 3-year-old daughter, three embryos that we have given back to Jesus and two we still long to meet.

Tom and Stacy, Washington

Our story to parenthood is simple. After several failed IVF attempts, we began to contemplate traditional adoption. We were comfortable with the idea of growing our family without requiring a genetic connection and simply wanted to be parents and share our love. After completing a traditional adoption process (home study, background checks, classes, etc.), we began to survey our options: adoption from abroad, locally, via foster care, etc. But none of them resonated with us; the uncertainties involved and potential risks seemed too great. Just at that moment, online research led us to EASCP. Maria had just started the program, and since we had already completed a home study, we were able to move swiftly and smoothly forward with a match. We were matched with our wonderful donor family, and soon a frozen embryo transfer occurred that resulted in our son, Julian. Experiencing the process of pregnancy and birth gave us a level of control over the pre-natal environment that was

What Other Families Are Saying...

comforting, as well as an immediate, strong connection to our child. Making the leap from infertility to a traditional adoption can be daunting, for a whole host of reasons. So much so, it may cause couples to abandon the dream of parenthood. Embryo adoption provides a wonderful alternative path to growing your family, offering many of the attributes of a traditional pregnancy with far less uncertainty than a traditional adoption, all at a reasonable cost. We are thrilled to have our little boy and can't imagine a world without him. Thank you, Maria, for making it possible.

Brian and Melanie, Illinois

We knew in our hearts that further treatment was not for us, and after much prayer, we decided to look at embryo adoption. We completed the application process and were so excited when Maria found a match for us. Looking over the information required a lot of prayer, but we knew God had this family for us. We're now seven months pregnant, and we cannot tell you the joy that God is bringing into our lives. Already we feel so blessed to have this opportunity. The baby is kicking as I write this! Embryo adoption is a choice for life and about life. We hope you're greatly blessed by this book.

Brian and Steva, Iowa

Souls on Ice

A Letter To Our Precious Loves:

It is with a heavy heart that we write you this letter. Although we've never met you, we feel a close connection to you. We love you with all our heart, and that love allowed us to do the hardest thing ever — give you away. Never did we want to give you away, but after a very traumatic childbirth, Marissa physically couldn't bring you into this world. We gave you away to give you a chance at life because that's what you deserve. Although it is heartbreaking knowing we will never get to hold and love you, to comfort you and be there for you and watch you grow up, we trust in the Heavenly Father's plan. He has a grand purpose for your life. He will take good care of you and use all this sadness and turn it into joy by blessing another Godly couple with a family. Our hearts are overjoyed that this amazing couple, Bethany and Chris, will be your Mommy and Daddy. We know they will be such loving, nurturing, wonderful parents and that they will teach you about your Heavenly Father. Our prayer is that you will be raised to know and love the Lord with all your heart, soul, mind and strength. We pray that you live a good, happy, blessed life. If you would ever like to meet us or inquire about your biological and half-siblings, our arms are wide open. We would be overjoyed. It is here where we must say goodbye. We can't go on this journey with you, so ... because of our great love for you, we are releasing you into the Almighty Father's Arms of Love, trusting his perfect will for your lives. Never forget how deeply loved and special you are. You will ALWAYS be in

What Other Families Are Saying ...

our thoughts and prayers and hold a special place in our hearts.

Love, Marvin and Marissa, Michigan

"Children, too, are a gift from the Lord,
the fruit of the womb, a reward." (Psalm 127:3)

Resources

Information about Embryo Adoption Services of Cedar Park

www.AdoptEmbryos.org
www.DonateEmbryos.org
1-888-959-7712

Embryo Adoption Services of Cedar Park is a ministry of Cedar Park Church ...
... Dedicated to Uniting Families for Life!

About Us:

- Services are available nationwide, and internationally on a case-by-case basis
- We are a Christian organization
- Prefer couples are married three years
- Contact options are: closed, open, semi-open or contact through Cedar Park only
- Home study required, social worker available to come to you anywhere in the United States
- Age limit female — 48
- Facilitate matching between donating and adopting families
- Provide legal contracts for both families, donating and adopting

- Contract assistance for families who find their own match
- We arrange for the transportation of embryos
- Adopting families can use their own fertility doctor
- We facilitate coordination between clinics
- We provide all documentation for clinics as required by the FDA

What is embryo donation and embryo adoption, and how does it work?

- Many couples who undergo fertility treatments have embryos remaining after they complete treatments and build their family.

- Hundreds of thousands of frozen embryos are now held in suspended animation in freezers at fertility clinics around the country, creating a dilemma for the couples who created them and need to decide the fate of their potential offspring.

- Nearly one in four couples struggles with infertility. These couples desire, more than anything, a child of their own to love, nurture and raise.

- In some cases, a woman may be capable of a successful pregnancy, but unable to conceive. Because another couple's embryo can be transferred into her womb, she

Resources

could adopt an embryo and give birth to her own adopted child.

- These embryos can now have a chance to be born into a loving family and bring great joy to those that have suffered with infertility. Placing/donating families will have the assurance they need to give the gift of life to another couple.

- Embryo Adoption Services of Cedar Park offers both adopting parents and placing families a chance to find each other and to give children a chance at life.

What does Embryo Adoption Services of Cedar Park provide?

- Phone consultations to answer your questions regarding embryo donation and embryo adoption and guidance and resources for a well-informed decision-making process.

- Matching prospective families looking to donate and adopt embryos.

- Coordination of the legal and physical transfer of embryos between fertility clinics working with the donating and adopting families.

- Referrals to social workers and counselors.

- A mentor family that has already gone through the process, so you have an experienced support system during your embryo adoption journey.

- Baby shower and/or a special gift from us when each child is born.

- Opportunities to meet other families through group events, such as barbecues, Christmas parties or birthday celebrations.

- Confidential and permanent recordkeeping.

- Liaison between the donating/adopting families for future reference or contact, if desired.

- Facilitating communication between donor and adopting families after babies are born.

- We are *committed* to praying for you and your family!

For the Donating Couple:

If you have remaining embryos stored in the freezer, you might be facing a dilemma. Perhaps you have finished building your family, are not able to care for more

Resources

children or are not physically able to carry your frozen embryos to term. You have the following options:

1. Continue to keep them stored for a later transfer and future family building.
2. Discard the embryos.
3. Donate the embryos for research if they are eligible.
4. Donate the embryos to another family through the process of embryo adoption.

We hope that you would consider making your embryos available for a waiting adopting family! At Embryo Adoption Services of Cedar Park (EASCP), the level of contact between adopting and donating families is agreed upon by the donor family and the adopting family. Here are some basic types of contact through our program:

1. *Anonymous. No Direct Contact.* Donors can still be informed when a child is born, but there is no other communication.

2. *Open through Cedar Park.* We provide each couple with the other couple's first names only, with pictures and letters redirected through us. Donor couples receive a birth announcement, photos and updates at least once a year, but not limited to once a year. (We think this is the best way to start.)

3. *Totally Open.* You are known to each other through first and last names, you have each other's addresses and contact each other directly. This is generally what happens after families have been "open through Cedar Park" first. We are available to help facilitate this step.

The process begins by providing information about you and your embryos. We begin searching for a potential match by providing family profiles for you to review and consider. Your embryos remain your embryos until we have sent you an adopting family profile that you are comfortable selecting. We send information about you to the adopting family based upon the contact option you desire. If the adoption family is satisfied, we then have a match.

Program Requirements for Adopting Couples:

- Couples should be married three years or longer. We can be flexible to a degree on this, but would need to discuss your particular situation.

- Couples are required to complete a home study or home evaluation. We have a social worker that can come to you, anywhere in the United States.

- Home studies include background checks, financial stability verification, some basic counseling (regarding raising adopted children), a home visit by a social worker and letters of recommendation. Additional information may be required to complete your home study.

- Couples may be required to attend classes on raising adopted children. These classes are generally available locally.

- We have social workers available for you. Phone appointments are possible and encouraged. Deciding what kind of contact you would like to have with a donating/placing family is a central issue, for example, affecting the child for the rest of his or her life. The decision can evolve and change, but obviously must be agreed upon by both families. Your position on this vital step will determine the families on your list of potential matches. We have found that relationships can evolve over time. We can discuss this with you.

- The woman will need a letter from her fertility doctor stating that there are no contraindications to pregnancy and that her health would support pregnancy, childbirth and parenting. She should also be current with her regular Pap test and mammogram, as well, if indicated by her physician. It is helpful and best to be close to a normal BMI for a healthy pregnancy.

Souls on Ice

- We believe every embryo is a human life. When thawing and transferring embryos, we require that no more embryos be transferred than what the woman would be willing to carry to term, and no more than two embryos transferred at a time, unless the embryos are already frozen in straws of three. (We will have more information for you and your doctor to discuss regarding thawing and transferring of embryos.) Recent findings suggest that transferring one embryo can have very similar successful live birth rates as transferring more than one. You can discuss this with your fertility doctor. Multiple births are not desired, nor should they be planned for, as they increase risks in the pregnancy.

For the Adopting Family:

If you are interested in having a child (or children) and embryo adoption seems like the option for you, we are so excited for you! Embryo adoption is a wonderful way to add to your family, whether you've struggled with infertility or you've already had children of your own. Here are some steps to get you started:

<u>Step One</u>: Secure a letter from your doctor stating that you have no contraindications to pregnancy.
<u>Step Two</u>: Our agency conducts a home study. Just like any standard adoption, we require a home study before we can place any embryos with a family.

Resources

<u>Step Three</u>: Create a book of photos and family information to share with a prospective donating family.

<u>Step Four</u>: It's a match! Once we have matched you with a donating family, we fly the embryos to your doctor's clinic to be transferred to your womb. At EASCP, we handle your paperwork, fly the embryos if necessary and act as a liaison between you and your donating family.

Please don't hesitate to contact us. We would be glad to answer your questions.

For more information or an application packet
call 888-959-7712
e-mail maria@adoptembryos.org
or visit
www.adoptembryos.org
www.donateembryos.org

Additional Internet Resources

Embryo Adoption Awareness Campaign:
www.EmbryoAdoption.org

Webinar Archives From the Embryo Adoption Awareness Center — a very comprehensive list (There is lots of information here about "Talking to Your Children" and "What to Tell Your Children" and many more topics for you to browse)
http://www.embryoadoption.org/education/Webinar-Archives.cfm

Souls on Ice

General FAQ Information About Embryo Adoption (This is not specific for EASCP necessarily, this is general information)
http://www.embryoadoption.org/education/Webinar-Archives.cfm

General FAQ Information About Embryo Donation (This is not specific for EASCP necessarily, this is general information)
http://www.embryoadoption.org/faqs/donors.cfm

General Definition of Terms/Glossary
http://www.embryoadoption.org/faqs/glossary.cfm

Laws by State Regarding Embryo Adoption
https://nightlightevents.webex.com/nightlightevents/lsr.php?AT=pb&SP=EC&rID=5371482&rKey=dfff84cc3fdc6638

Listings of Other Agencies Nationwide
http://www.embryoadoption.org/adoption_agencies/embryo_adoption_services_matrix.cfm

Books

Hope & Will Have a Baby: The Gift of Embryo Donation
by Irene Celcer

Before You Were Born ... Our Wish for a Baby
by Janice Grimes

A Blessing From Above
by Patti Henderson

Resources

Embryo Donation and Embryo Adoption:
Loving Choices for Christians
by Jon D. Van Regenmorter and
Sylvia A. Van Regenmorter

Information for Catholics

Information for Catholics Regarding Embryo Adoption
www.catholic.org/featured/headline.php?ID=2236&page=2

Catholic Moral Theology Article
http://catholicmoraltheology.com/setting-the-captives-free-is-there-precedent-for-embryo-adoption-in-scripture-and-medieval-christian-tradition/

Webinar Discussion Regarding Embryo Adoption for Catholics
https://nightlightevents.webex.com/nightlightevents/lsr.php?AT=pb&SP=EC&rID=5371482&rKey=dfff84cc3fdc6638

The Catholic Case for Embryo Adoption
http://www.lifenews.com/2011/04/17/the-catholic-case-for-embryo-adoption/

For more information on reaching your city with stories from your church or organization, go to www.testimonybooks.com.

GOOD CATCH
PUBLISHING

Did one of these stories touch you?
Did one of these real people move you to tears?
Tell us (and them) about it on our Facebook page at www.facebook.com/GoodCatchPublishing.